Contents

Foreword

As an educational publisher for more than 12 years, I have had the remarkable privilege of engaging with some of the leading thinkers on the educational scene in the UK and beyond. It has always been, and continues to be a humbling experience. However, bringing the thinking of our authors to a wider audience of teachers and school managers has never been sufficient in itself; more important is to explore the application of that thinking, so that it can have classroom relevance and impact.

One important educational area that has always been difficult to tackle is that of creativity. In 2005 we had the idea of bringing together four of the most creative educational minds we knew to see what would happen. This book is the first outcome of their collective thinking. The series of meetings between the authors of this book were some of the liveliest and most inspirational events I have attended, as I watched the creative enthusiasm build on itself. As a result this is a book vibrant in its style and unique in its structure.

Each of the authors has already established a substantial reputation as a highly acclaimed practitioner with both children and adult audiences. In particular they have all, in their different ways, demonstrated keen insight into both current and established research, which they use to underpin the practical experiences they recommend in their presentations. This book is a small accumulation of these insights presented for other practitioners to absorb and then make their own.

One common thesis to which all the authors subscribe is the importance of narrative as a powerful vehicle for carrying deep learning experiences, and hence each author's section is introduced by a compelling story to illustrate this concept. This is followed by a section of theory that underpins the practical classroom exercises that complete each author's section.

To my mind the outcome is a powerful collection of ideas and concepts useful to any teacher who wishes to reflect on some of the different ways in which the creative minds of their students may be engaged to make their learning more powerful – whatever the subject and whatever the level. Dip into this book and allow your own creativity to flourish and your own pedagogy to be transformed.

Jim Houghton, January 2007
Managing Director, NEP, 1993-2006

Preface

Carl Jung believed there to be four primary modes of seeing the world: two rational functions – thinking and feeling; and two perceptive functions – sensation and intuition. Thinking is analytical, deductive cognition; feeling is synthetic, all-inclusive cognition. Sensation is the perception of facts; intuition is the perception of the unseen. In each person there is a degree of all four but, as individuals, we all have our own individual preferences.

We, the authors, are no different. This work would not have come to fruition were it not that each of us recognizes the partiality of our own way of seeing the world and is open to understanding how others see. And although we may vary individually in our acceptance of Jung's beliefs, his ideas have provided us as a group with a model for developing and expressing the ideas in this book.

It is not far off the mark to say that we four authors, while happy to explore and engage at all four levels, each have our own primary mode way of seeing the world, and you, our reader, may see this in our writings. But we have sought in common to explore each mode in setting down the ideas, principles and practices that inspire our teaching. It is for this reason that each of our sections covers three distinct areas:

> Story – feeling and emotion
>
> Theory – thinking and logic
>
> Exercises – sensation and practice

The link that binds the process and delivery throughout the whole work is intuition. While we each have our preferred approaches we share an intuitive belief that the lessons included in this work are worth revisiting, relearning and reapplying.

This book has been structured to engage, inspire and inform. The challenge in any learning is to feel confident enough about where you are already that you feel able to move on and explore areas that may not be known and that may challenge your preferences and view of the world. We hope that each person reading this will be both reassured, by engaging in at least one section that appeals to their perception of the world, and also challenged, in applying themselves to other sections that may not be their immediate preference.

We hope that it will be possible for you, our reader, to enter this book at any point and to find there ideas and practices that will inspire your teaching. There is something of a progression in the layout of this book, in that it moves from looking in the beginning at more general aspects of creativity and learning to more focused investigations of specific aspects of a creative curriculum. Equally, however, each section contains within itself ideas that inform the whole structure of the book, and could serve as well to open the book as any other. We hope that you enjoy your journey through this book as much as we have enjoyed our journey together in creating it.

Steve Bowkett
Trisha Lee
Roy Leighton
Tim Harding

The man who painted clouds

Steve Bowkett

Kai set out to walk to his work. He had done this every day for forty years. His simple hut was built close to the stream that passed through the village. Today, since the spring rains had brought mud downstream, the water ran brown. And there was a frothy scum on it from where the villagers had washed their clothes and their pots and their pans. In Kai's language the name of the village meant 'The settlement that stands beside the clear stream'. Kai smiled to think that the world changes anyway, even if sometimes words do not.

His journey took him along the line of the valley to the town at the foot of the hills. Beyond those hills rose great mountains of blue-grey rock, and beyond them the northern province – the Jade Province – that Kai had never visited, but dreamed about often. In Kai's language the name of the town meant 'The place surrounded by forest'. Now though the trees had mostly vanished, cut down to make way for the shanties and the factories that had brought such wealth to some of the people in the area. Many of the workers lived in the shanties, and this made Kai feel sorry for them and glad for himself to have his own place in the peaceful village 'beside the clear stream'.

Kai worked in one of the factories in the town. The factory produced paintings that were sold mainly to the city dwellers in the Jade Province and the Emerald Province, which was Kai's own region. Many copies of each painting were made. The procedure for manufacturing them never varied.

The Master Painter (who for many years had been Lu Lun) created the first picture. Then an assembly line of tables was set up and the workers were put in their places. The first worker's job was to spread a delicate wash across the canvas. The second worker's task was to paint in the mountains. The third worker dabbed in the yellow sun – the same sun each and every time, with no deviation in the way the paint

was applied. The fourth worker, using a finer brush, put some birds in the sky; the same birds in the same sky, each time. Kai – the ninth worker in line – was the man who painted clouds. This had been his task for the best part of his life, since his youth when he was ambitious and full of grand dreams.

At the end of the assembly line sat Lu Lun who, as a finished painting came to him, signed the canvas with a proud flourish, varying his signature minutely each time. This meant that Ch'un, the factor owner, could sell the paintings for a higher price as original works of art.

As Kai waited this morning for the first of the incomplete paintings to reach him, he noticed that a young boy was sitting beside him, in the place of old Ssu-Ma Ch'en. Upon enquiring, Kai learned that the boy's name was Tso Chan, and this was his very first day at the picture factory.

"But what of Ssu-Ma Ch'en?" Kai asked. The boy's face saddened.

"I am sorry sir, but Huc, the Overseer, told me that he died. It seems his soul passed on as he sat watching the sunset last evening. His body was found beside the Ancient Pine in the hills. They say he had tears on his face. Perhaps he was sorry to be leaving life…"

"Perhaps," said Kai very quietly. Or perhaps, he thought, perhaps he wept for never having lived it.

The dawn had been sunny and bright, but as the hours wore on the sky clouded and the wind turned round and blew from the north. Kai's heart darkened also, feeling heavy in mourning for old Ssu-Ma Ch'en – the man who painted stones – and heavier too for Tso Chan, the young boy who had taken up his task.

8

Eventually some lamps were lit in the factory. Shortly afterwards Tso Chan found himself in trouble with Huc the Overseer.

"Look at that!" stormed Huc, whose authority was vested in fear. "Look, you have painted the stones differently in these two pictures. Are you not paying attention boy?"

"Well…" Tso Chan, despite his trembling, found the courage to speak. "I was getting bored sir— "

"Bored!" Huc thundered, as though he had heard a blasphemy. "That is not the point. You are not here to be interested in anything, child, but to paint stones – the same stones in the same way on every canvas. This noble task has been handed down to you by others wiser and more experienced than you are. You should be grateful and humbled to receive such privilege!"

"I thought," said Tso Chan timidly, "that I would learn more by trying things differently, just a little perhaps…"

Huc's voice became very quiet. He put his face close to Tso Chan's. "You will learn by doing as you are told. Ssu-Ma Ch'en spent his life understanding that lesson. Respect his memory and respect the greatness of Lu Lun, whose original work is a template for your understanding. Do not dare, ever again, to deviate from the ways of the Master. Is that clear?"

Tso Chan remained silent, his eyes lowered. Huc stepped away.

"Then get on with your work and I will forget your stupidity this once."

The assembly line had come to a stop while Huc admonished the boy. Now at a nod from the Overseer, things moved again. Kai painted clouds and passed the canvas to Tso Chan, who painted stones just as Huc had instructed him. And Kai noticed that tears sparkled in Tso Chan's eyes. The same tears, Kai guessed, as the ones they said were in the eyes of old Ssu-Ma Ch'en on the day that life had left him beside the Ancient Pine.

As noon approached, the wind outside blustered even harder and gusted through the space where the workers toiled. The dusty lamps swung on their chains and beads rattled suddenly at the window panes.

Kai was startled out of his stupor. "Look!" he cried. "Look hailstones – let's rush out!"

Forgetting himself he jumped from his bench and ran outside, marvelling and wondering at the huge dark power of the stormclouds, delighted by the sting of the icy crystals on his face. He heard laughter beside him and saw that Tso Chan was the only one to have followed him. The boy's face was uptilted to the sky and his eyes, squinting into the hailstorm, were full of energy and light.

9

They danced together, the old man and the young boy, while the storm played out above them and thunder boomed about the heavens. The danced and danced until Kai's bones grew tired and he had to stop. But his heart was still as light as the air and there was a feeling inside him that he remembered from his youth; a passion that had burned there before he ever saw the town or the factory or his place ninth in line at the table.

He looked at Tso Chan and knew that the boy was feeling the same. Tso Chan's face shone with excitement. "*What is it Kai?*" He put a hand to his heart. "What is it called?"

And the answer came to Kai in no time at all, as though it had always been there.

"Firstness."

Because of their disobedience in getting out of line both Kai and Tso Chan lost their jobs. In the early afternoon, by which time the storm had passed, they could be seen wandering through the outskirts of the town 'surrounded by forest', not knowing quite what to do…

Until Kai had an idea. He said, "What do you most want to do with your life?"

"I want to be a painter," Tso Chan replied with no hesitation, "more than anything else."

"And you will, I daresay, want to paint stones now and then…"

Tso Chan chuckled, until he realized that Kai was being serious.

"To paint stones you must *know* stones. Now then, I wonder where we will find lots and lots of stones?"

A slow smile grew across Kai's wrinkled features and he pointed. Tso Chan followed the direction of the finger and looked up at the vastness of the blue-grey mountains. His face fell.

"But however will we get there Kai?"

The old man took a step and another step and a third step… And Tso Chan was answered.

They climbed through the long afternoon, enjoying the sun, marvelling at the colours of the mountain flowers. Tso Chan stopped often to pick up stones and turn them this way and that in his hands. Kai was grateful for these opportunities to rest. He lay on the grass and gazed at the clouds and let their cloudness soak into his soul. They were all different, he noticed, and ever changing. How could he ever have painted them

when they were so subtle and fleeting and so unique?

Soon afterwards the two friends continued on their way, until Kai realized that the clouds seemed to be no nearer. He mentioned this to Tso Chan, adding, "So how can I ever hope to know them?"

The boy shrugged lightly. "They will be no farther away down in the valley," he suggested. And Kai smiled at this green wisdom.

On the return journey Kai offered to visit Tso Chan's home and apologize to the boy's parents. "They had always wanted me to work in the picture factory," Tso Chan explained. "They say they were never clever enough to do that. They wanted me to succeed, so they could be proud of me."

Kai nodded but inside he felt angry and wondered what the anger was telling him.

They arrived back at the town late in the afternoon, by which time the sun had sunk beyond the foothills and a full moon, tinted the faintest pearl, had risen. Tso Chan was still busy worrying about what his parents would say, but Kai's attention was fixed on a wispy cloud that had appeared from nowhere and now drifted across the moon's round face.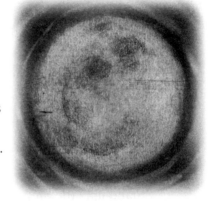

A spark leapt in the old man's mind. For the moon, he thought, there is the cloud. And for the stones there is the grass. And for the grass there are the open spaces. And for the open spaces there are the mountains. And for the mountains there is the sky. And for the sky there is the moon…

He turned to the boy. "Tso Chan, my new friend. It occurs to me that our shift at the factory – were we still there – would not be finishing for several hours yet. Your parents will not expect you home for quite some time."

"But I must face their disappointment—"

"Or make sure there is no disappointment to face, but only the pride they have in you already."

"How can I achieve that?" Tso Chan wondered.

Kai shrugged lightly. "Let's paint," he suggested.

So they went instead to Kai's hut in the village. Tso Chan was delighted to see his friend's fine collection of brushes and paints. But they were hardly used. "I have been so busy painting bits of the picture that I never…" A sharpness caught in Kai's throat and his eyes gleamed. "I never dared to try it all."

"Let's dare now," Tso Chan said. And he picked up a brush.

Kai had one big blank canvas propped against the back wall of his hut. And there they painted firstness; the cloudness of cloud, the stone-ness of stones, the essence of the moon and the simple happiness that was in their own hearts. Each blade of grass was different and distinct. Each cloud and each stone spoke its own unique self. The two friends lost themselves in the work and found themselves there by the time the oil in the lamps had burned out and the painting was as finished as it ever could be.

Then Kai and Tso Chan slept contentedly on the floor where they had laid down their brushes. The moon followed its path through the stars and a cool wind swept gently off the mountains and stirred the long golden grass on the hills.

Upon waking the young boy and the old man found that a small crowd of villagers had gathered at the threshold, straining and bustling to catch sight of the painting that one of them had earlier noticed. Kai was too sleepy to send them away, and Tso Chan was embarrassed for his work to be put under such close scrutiny. But the murmuring of the people was excited, and their delight was sincere when a neighbour's cat, wandering in, leapt at a butterfly realized by four childlike strokes of Kai's brush on the canvas.

Word of the picture spread quickly. And by the wonderful tumbling of the dice of circumstance Ch'un the factory owner was drawn by curiosity to Kai's hut on the same day that the Emperor happened to be passing through the valley on his way to the capital.

Ch'un, indeed everyone present, bowed humbly in the Emperor's presence. Tso Chan bowed too, but secretly glanced up and was pleased to see kindness and wisdom in the great man's face.

"Stand up," the Emperor commanded. The people stood. He put out his hand and his subjects stood aside… But only Kai understood. For the Emperor had seen the painting and was reaching as though to touch it – No, *as though to walk into it…*

"I thought…" The Emperor's voice was a whisper. "I thought this was another valley, somewhere I had never been. A perfect, secret, unspoiled place…"

"It is as perfect as the full moon's face," Kai said gently. The Emperor nodded slowly.

"But I see it is this valley in the early times, in the first times before people ever came here."

"I will buy it!" Ch'un interrupted, reaching for his money pouch. "You are obviously a great painter Kai, a Grand Master. I will buy it and my workers will make a thousand copies – a hundred thousand! – so that his Mightiness the Emperor's subjects all across the land might marvel at its brilliance! I will get rid of Lu Lun and you, Kai, can sit at your ease and sign the pictures as they reach the end of the line."

"I will have none of that." The Emperor's voice had an edge of steel and Ch'un

12

was cowed. He turned to Kai and Tso Chan. "The painting will stay here. If anyone wants to see it they must make the journey themselves." He smiled. "But I notice that while you are far wealthier than I am in some ways, you want for certain comforts. I would like to reward you, Kai and Tso Chan, however you wish…"

"I wish," said Kai, "that I might live out the rest of my days making more paintings."

"That's my wish too," chipped in Tso Chan. He pointed at Kai. "I wish to learn to paint wonderfully, like my friend."

"Learn first," Kai said, "that your learning is in the hand with which you are pointing."

So it came to be. Kai and Tso Chan created their pictures, each one different, and their childlike hearts were glad through all the days of their lives. And now and again the Emperor made the journey to see that first painting that they had created together, and it was always new for him and he was always moved by wonder.

But neither Kai nor Tso Chan ever told him that the painting showed the valley, not as it was long ago, but how it would be one day when the people had gone on their greater journey; when the great blue-grey mountains were a little older but the wind still whispered through the grass.

And here now, look, the full moon rises and is reflected in a puddle from this evening's rain. And the stillness of the water is not broken. And the moon does not get wet.

Creativity and how we think

Steve Bowkett

Theories

In the mid-1970s the American psychologist Julian Jaynes suggested in his remarkable book *The Origin of Consciousness in the Breakdown of the Bicameral Mind* (1990) that ancient peoples lacked a sense of personal identity and the ability to be aware of internal dialogues. In other words, pre-Homeric man (Jaynes uses Homeric literature to support his ideas) experienced the world directly and was not 'aware of being aware', which is one sometimes useful definition of consciousness. He expounds the notion that the voices of God or the gods were intuitions arising from the minds of ordinary individuals – auditory hallucinations emanating from what we now often call the subconscious. And yet they were full of wisdom and ideas that the recipients 'didn't know they knew' before that moment.

Jaynes's theories were and remain controversial. Indeed, we still do not possess any overall agreement about the nature (let alone the purpose) of consciousness – in philosophy, this is known as the 'hard problem'. But as educationalists our stock-in-trade is ideas: the content of the curriculum is made up of them, and how well our students make sense of them is a measure of their success as learners. Any insights that can help us to work with ideas – the raw material of education – are worth considering further, which is what this and my chapter on narrative intelligence aim to do.

Certainly, throughout the educational world there is an increasing emphasis on thinking skills and creativity, and any good teacher wants his or her students to be more than just vessels filled up with facts (which can become out of date with frightening speed). The late American entrepreneur Peter Drucker once said that the currency of the twenty-first century is ideas. People who can assimilate, manipulate and generate ideas in innovative ways are more likely to be employable, in more fields, than those who are simply literate, numerate and able to follow instructions. More than that: twenty years ago Colin Rose, in his seminal book *Accelerated Learning* (1985), raised our awareness of what 'learning to learn' implies. That phrase embodies an attitude as well as a repertoire of skills, and these are going to become more and more important as the pace of change in the world increases. A recent statistic claimed that 60 per cent of the jobs our current ten year olds will take up on leaving school do not even exist yet. Even if the percentage were much lower than this the notion itself is startling and surely a call to urgent action.

Many powerful voices in education advocate a creative thinking approach to teaching and learning. Some of the most persuasive reiterate wisdoms and strategies that have been known for a long time but forgotten perhaps in the frantic rush to raise standards through top-down, content-led methods of schooling that emphasize the reaching of levels and the hitting of targets.

Whether Jaynes's theories are true or not, he succeeds in highlighting the idea that some (or even most) of our mental processing occurs without our realizing it, and has done for thousands of years. These days we commonly refer to this by talking about the conscious and the subconscious mind.

Our conscious thinking is composed of thoughts that we know we are having (or 'making' might be a better word) *as we make them*, for reasons that we largely understand. And, by an act of will, we can change those conscious thoughts. The conscious thinking agenda is out in the open: we are aware of it and why, and can modify it when we want to. In other words we can make up our minds and change our minds directly and deliberately, as a consequence of our active self-aware reflection.

The conscious 'arena' that constitutes our 'awareness-of-being-aware' has been called cognitive space. Here the spotlight of our conscious attention shines on what we are doing mentally. The kinds of thinking going on in cognitive space include reasoning and evaluating, sequencing and prioritizing, comparing and contrasting. These and other so-called 'critical thinking skills' build towards our ability to construct narratives and arguments, solve problems and make decisions. These are the kinds of thinking (together with retaining and reiterating factual material on demand) traditionally emphasized and supposedly measured in schools (see Bellanca and Fogarty, 1986).

However, these are only some of the thinking tools in the mental toolbox. Other and more creative kinds of thinking (that is those generative of new ideas) have their roots in subconscious mental processing. This is to say, we all have the potential to process information, perhaps with the aim in mind of solving problems, making decisions and so on, without consciously doing all the work – although of course it's useful if we notice the outcomes of subconscious activity. Put simply, any truly effective creative thinking approach to learning must acknowledge our subconscious abilities and apply strategies for using them more effectively.

But what exactly is 'creativity'? There is no single, overarching definition (see Bowkett, 1997[1]), but I do think that creativity involves four important elements:

1   *noticing* – being observant about things happening externally, and noticing what's going on inside our own heads (this is fashionably called 'metacognition');

2   *questioning* – developing 'quality questioning' strategies, recognizing that many kinds of questions exist, like fine instruments set out in a box – we pick the right instrument for the right job;

3   *linking* – making links in the mind that we've not made before, building more complex structures from simpler, perhaps previously unconnected, ideas; this is the basis of turning knowledge into information (or, rather, in-formation – the active formation of greater understandings);

4   *multiple perspectives* – the willingness and ability to look at experience and ideas from different viewpoints (so-called 'thinking outside the box').

In our willingness to be like this, we are adopting an attitude. To me, this is the creative attitude. When I work with young children I tell them that to have lots of good ideas you need to be nosy – to notice what's going on around you and what's going on inside your head, and be happy to play with these ideas and change them. Since we are all naturally nosy, and since younger children still take joy in, as John Abbot and Terry Ryan say, 'creating naïve theories of everything', students can feel on safe and familiar ground from the outset.[2]

The creative attitude drives our ability to make sense of the world. Each moment, impressions pour into the brain, and this material has to be processed – to some extent consciously, but to a much larger extent subconsciously. We are constantly weaving a complex network of associations that create an understanding of what the world is like and how we fit into it. This network (the ultimate in-formation in our heads) is often called the 'map of reality', and forms the vital resource of memory.

Another vital resource is that of imagination, our ability to create mental impressions and structures that need have nothing to do with our immediate circumstances. Through imagination we can, as has been said, 'break the shackles of time and space'. People can create these structures ('make up their minds') and modify them ('change their minds') more or less deliberately. One goal of a creative thinking approach to education must surely be to enable students to use their imaginative powers more knowingly, insightfully and incisively.

This is borne out by the American psychologist Abraham Maslow, in his paper called 'Self-Actualizing People: A Study of Psychological Health' (1950).[3] He found that psychologically healthy people tend to be creative, and vice versa. They often experienced moments of illumination (that is, frequently had new ideas and insights) accompanied by feelings of delight, joy, excitement and so on. I suggest that this is what inspiration is all about: to be inspired is to experience sudden new realizations accompanied by pleasurable feelings. Maslow called them 'peak experiences' (PEs). Maslow further suggested that PEs occur naturally in human beings whose 'deficiency needs' (food, warmth, security, sex, and so on) have been satisfied. In other words, we are all born with the potential to think creatively, but that potential is only developed to a high degree in the right nurturing environment. When Maslow discussed PEs with his students he and they were startled and pleased to realize that not only could they recall many more previous PEs that they had not noticed at the time but also experienced more of them from then on – and increasingly at will. Self-actualizing people don't have to 'wait for inspiration to strike', but can have new ideas whenever they want to. When students have reached this level of capability I think that we as teachers can begin to feel that we've achieved the primary goal of education. When our students are encouraged to express their increasingly informed theories about the world, and when we value the outcomes of their thinking, the students are 'reared up' to be independent and creative thinkers – self-actualizing people.

Towards the end of the nineteenth century the French mathematician Henri Poincaré identified four stages in the creative process:[4]

1 First the mental ground needs to be prepared. The *preparation* stage occurs formally through schooling, where tasks, activities and strategies are employed that focus students' thinking. But we also prepare in the most informal of ways simply through our daily experiences. As we grow and mature our preparation for creative thought – for the generation of new insights and ideas – follows the path of our developing interests in life.

2 Once the creative soil is prepared, we *assimilate* material in a more concentrated way both consciously and subconsciously – we till and tend the ground. This stage (also called the stage of incubation) includes the more conscious activities of deliberate research, brainstorming and reflecting on the material we're working with. But we also mull over ideas, slip into sometimes quite extended daydreams,

17

'sleep on' the problem or task and sometimes wake up with new insights. As the assimilation of information proceeds, the generation of ideas gathers pace.

3   When a new idea is recognized – when it enters cognitive space – we experience an 'aha!' or 'Eureka!' moment. Poincaré called these moments of *illumination*. Continuing with our soil metaphor, illuminations occur when the seeds of our (usually subconscious) thinking break through into the light of day. Such insights occur at all levels of detail. A novelist might suddenly have an idea for a whole new story, or perhaps just realize that his main character must wear glasses, for reasons that suddenly become clear.

4   Poincaré proposed that the final stage of the creative cycle is *verification*. Once we've had our new ideas we need to find out how useful they are likely to be. Part of the self-actualizing process is to 'know deep down' that an idea will work. A novelist who's just thought of a new story will immediately and spontaneously have a cascade of further ideas that begin to demonstrate the potential of the initial insight. There will also be that sense of excitement and positive anticipation in the work to come. Verification also involves the more conscious critical thinking skills of evaluating, prioritizing and so on, and testing ideas against other people's thinking. The novelist partly verifies the achievement of her story by the impact it makes on her readers.

Obviously the notions of conscious and subconscious thinking, of memory and imagination and the 'four stages' of creativity are simplistic and artificial. The mind is a seething ocean of thoughts, complex beyond our current understanding. To best utilize this incredible energy in making sense of what has been called 'the chaos of experience' perhaps we might follow Einstein's advice as we build our strategies towards a creative curriculum:

Out of clutter find simplicity. From discord find harmony. In the middle of difficulty, find opportunity.

Implications and applications

The Disney strategy

One immediate application of Poincaré's insights can be found in what has come to be known as the *Disney strategy*. This might be more accurately thought of as a 'meta-strategy' since it seems to accommodate the learning styles and preferences of most students through the creative cycle.

Apparently Walt Disney, whose creativity and entrepreneurial skills were prodigious, would daydream a lot during the early phases of an idea's development. Imagine him sitting in that quiet, inward-gazing state asking questions such as 'What if I could build a fairyland city where people from all across the world could come and enjoy themselves and meet Mickey and Pluto and Donald? What if–?'

This, naturally enough, is known as the *dreamer phase* of the strategy, although I emphasize that the daydreaming is systematic and not of the 'idle' kind. Systematic daydreaming occurs when we deliberately enter this particular mental state for specific purposes and reasons we decide upon earlier. This gives us time to assimilate and prepare – to preprocess the task – so that as we sit quietly noticing the thoughts that rise up from the subconscious mind we recognize them as trains of thought and not disconnected fragments. Idle daydreaming tends to occur spontaneously, for no particular reason except perhaps to disengage from the hubbub of the outside world. This sort of 'brain break' does recharge the batteries and refresh the concentration, however, allowing us to return to conscious thinking tasks with greater energy and focus.

Thoughts arise quite randomly during idle daydreaming, and we might find ourselves 'thought-hopping', following vague associations from one scenario to the next. In both idle and systematic daydreaming, though, the brain produces electrical impulses known as alpha waves.[5] We are in 'alpha state' when we are consciously settled, with the gateway to the subconscious open wide, with 'divided awareness' such that we can clearly notice our thoughts but also have the presence of mind to articulate them and respond to stimuli – questions, suggestions and so on – from outside sources.

One outcome of the dreamer phase of the Disney strategy is to envision the big picture, to create an overview of what the whole thing might be like and/or to explore alternative and ultimately incongruent or contradictory possibilities and outcomes.

With the 'grand dream' in mind, we then need to realize it – to make it a physical reality. So the next phase of the cycle is quite properly called the *realist phase*. During this period the creative subconscious flow of ideas continues but conscious critical thinking is brought to bear on it so that ideas can be assessed and a solid plan formulated. In terms of classroom tasks this is the 'doing time', when ideas are noted in a more organized way, when stories are written in first draft, when drawings are made and so on. Because new ideas continue to spring to mind during the flow of composition, material at this stage can look messy, littered with corrections, amendments and deletions. This is perfectly fine and a natural consequence of how the creative process works.

Once the work has been realized in this relatively raw form it needs to be refined by the creator, who now enters the *critic phase* of the Disney strategy. Big new ideas at this stage are not likely to be very helpful (or if they are compellingly so the painter or writer must go 'back to the drawing board' and more or less start again). In this mental state the creative flow dwindles to a trickle or stops completely and the work is regarded with the minimum of emotional involvement. This is an important point, because if the story,

19

painting or whatever is reviewed too emotionally it may cloud the logical judgement of the work. It's easy to conjure up the stereotypical scenario of the despairing artist tearing up his just-finished painting or the demoralized novelist throwing her manuscript disgustedly into the bin, vowing never to write another word again!

During the critic phase assessments are made coolly and reasonably. This is not to say that the student can't feel pleased with her achievement so far, nor that she mustn't rely upon intuition to help guide the reviewing procedure. In this sense, 'intuition' means 'inner tuition', noticing that a sentence (for example) 'just feels right', even if the writer can't explain the grammatical and syntactical rules that have created that balanced construction. The critic phase enables the outcomes of the work to be most useful and effective by considering these two powerful questions...

1   What changes will help this to be the best piece of work I can achieve?

2   What have I learned by doing this work that will help my next piece to be even better?

In a nutshell then, the Disney strategy boils down to Thinking time – Doing time – Reviewing time. This sounds like thorough common sense. And of course it is, but empowered by the insights of 'past models' defined and described by thinkers like Jaynes, Maslow, Poincaré and the rest. Fig. 1.1 illustrates how the Disney strategy overlaps with Poincaré's model of the creative cycle.

Fig 1.1   Poincare's creative cycle and the Disney strategy.

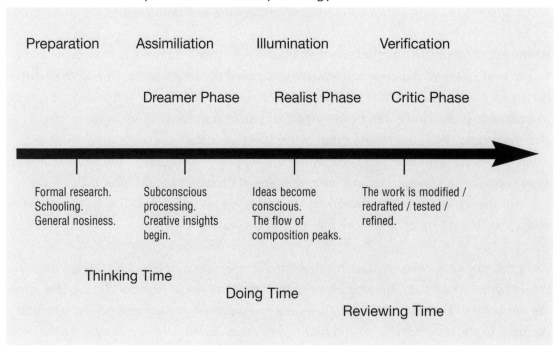

Both Poincaré's cycle and the Disney strategy have similarities to more recent models of the Accelerated Learning Cycle. Steve Minshull's *The Five Keys to Accelerated Learning* (2000), for instance, advises us:

1   Relax and focus your mind.

2   Map out the key points.

3   Organize relevant details.

4   Make associations (to enrich the work and explore alternative possibilities).

5   Revise regularly.

Examination of other 'learning cycles' will further verify the robustness and usefulness of the basic model.

Insight stones

I made the point earlier that more creative people – Maslow's self-actualizers – usually don't need to wait for inspiration to strike but can generate peak experiences at will. In other words, they can choose to have ideas at any time by firstly focusing the mind on the reasons for having the ideas, and then entering alpha state to notice their own systematic daydreams.

This is an easily teachable and learnable skill. One effective way of 'training alpha' is to use *anchoring techniques*.[6] In this sense an 'anchor' is a mental link (corresponding to a neural pathway) between the particular behaviour you want and something over which you have direct conscious control.

One anchor that I've found to be easily and effectively applied is the 'insight stone'. This is simply a small pebble or glass bead or marble which the student chooses for herself. If she's right-handed I suggest she begins by holding the stone in her left hand. The procedure for training alpha then proceeds like this:

● Decide what it is you're going to (systematically) daydream about.

● Tell yourself that when you decide to put the stone in your right hand, lots of interesting thoughts and good ideas will spring to mind – that is, make a clear statement of intent backed by a presupposition of success (the word 'will').

● Transfer the stone to your right hand and allow yourself to relax and settle.

● Begin to notice thoughts coming to mind. Begin to note these ideas in whatever form feels comfortable.

● As and when the flow of ideas thins out, break the state and end the daydream.

Many children in my experience take to the technique of insight stones quickly and easily. The 'knack' of developing this kind of insightfulness lies not in trying to consciously force

21

ideas into existence but simply in quietly noticing them as they appear in cognitive space. It's the subconscious part of the mind that does the work. Consciously we just maintain a state of 'relaxed alertness'.

Many children also speak in detail about the ideas they have, sometimes surprising themselves because 'I didn't know I knew that until I said it!'. This phenomenon is called *pole-bridging*. Information streaming across from the (more subconsciously processing) right cerebral hemisphere via the bundle of nerve fibres known as the corpus callosum into the (cognitive space of the) left hemisphere is consciously recognized for the first time. Children in effect enjoy extended peak experiences – moments or minutes of inspired thinking filled with ideas that are to them delightfully new. Your own role in this process would be to prompt and draw out further information through 'artfully vague' open questioning. *Artful vagueness* refers to the technique of giving the student a specific thinking task while leaving the outcomes vague. So, if the student as she holds the insight stone is visualizing a street, instead of asking 'Are there shops nearby?' – which prompts a yes/no answer in most cases – you might say 'Notice three interesting things nearby and tell me when you know more'. This usually results in much richer responses.[7]

Thinking tools digest

The notion of thinking 'tools' is a metaphor of course, which has some usefulness through association. Playing with metaphors is a powerful way of developing students' metacognitive abilities – more on that later. For now here is a list of commonly recognized kinds of thinking. As you peruse them, consider if and how and how much they are built into the teaching strategies you employ in the classroom. And feel free to alter any of the definitions in light of your own ideas.

- Analysing for assumption – 'teasing out' conclusions drawn in the absence of objective evidence, that is, those based on internal referents (of the material or those studying it).

- Analysing for bias – 'teasing out' subjective, personal points of view and how these may distort, delete and generalize the ideas in the material being studied.

- Associating – making links to create relationships and patterns, to map out a bigger picture.

- Attributing – attaching characteristics in order to describe, define or clarify.

- Brainstorming (or 'ideas cascading') – using the subconscious resource to help generate a 'melting pot' of ideas for further consideration.

- Classifying – sorting into groups based on common characteristics.

- Comparing/contrasting – finding differences and similarities.

- Decision making – making explicit an intention to act based upon reasoned consideration of a plan to resolve a problem.

- Deducing – creating an explanation or arriving at a conclusion based on the more objective gathering of outside evidence (that is, clues from the external world not generated subjectively within the mind).

- Determining cause and effect – clarifying logical-sequential relationships.

- Drawing conclusions – bringing consideration to an end by deducing and/or inferring from a body of information.

- Evaluating – judging or deciding upon the comparative worth, value or usefulness of something, by means which may be more or less conscious and explicit.

- Generalizing – broadening out a statement, viewpoint, and so on, from consideration of a limited number of particular cases.

- Handling ambiguity and paradox – reflecting on apparent contradictions/ conflicts/opposites and applying strategies as necessary to remain tolerant in the face of these.

- Hypothesizing – stating a possible position, situation, state, and so on, from an initial consideration of ideas; giving direction to further enquiry.

- Inferring – arriving at conclusions based upon a subjective assessment of information.

- Inventing – originating something as the product of creative and critical thinking.

- Personifying – associating/identifying with an object, creature, concept – investing it with your personal human qualities to achieve insight and further understanding.

- Predicting – using a range of strategies to anticipate possible outcomes.

- Prioritizing – creating an order/sequence according to predetermined values or attributes.

- Problem solving – selecting from a range of strategies to reach a desired state/resolve an issue/answer a question, and so on.

- Sequencing – creating an order based on the recognized attributes of items to be sequenced.

- Solving and making analogies – deepening understanding through the creation of comparisons based upon relational qualities.

- Visualizing – creating multisensory mental scenarios in cognitive space.

This is not an exhaustive list by any means, and represents just a fraction of the 'thinkings' that the mind can do. Consider these ('considering' being another mental skill): absorb, analyse, anticipate, apply, associate, attend, bisociate (and trisociate, quadrasociate, etc!),

23

categorize, choose, conclude, critique, deconstruct, describe, dissociate, discriminate, experiment, explain, feed back, integrate, judge, memorize, model, plan, pretend, rationalize, read, recite, recollect, reflect, reiterate, remember, reminisce, replan, research, speculate, synthesize, tell, verify… A surf through *Roget's Thesaurus* is likely to throw up plenty more.

Surface structure and deep structure

Language is revealing. This is an obvious thing to say, but the point is often missed and the power of the insight is not always exploited. If we consider our conscious thoughts to be the leaves and branches of the mental tree, subconscious thoughts are the roots – and to stretch the metaphor, the map of reality (memory) forms the soil out of which our thoughts, expressed partly through language, will grow.

What we say (or write) is what's visible 'on the surface' of our thinking. If I say 'I am hungry' that idea is now out in the open and apparently quite clear. But the words fail to reveal the total context in which they are embedded.[8] Questioning can draw out more information – How long has it been since you've eaten? Have you just noticed the smell of the cake shop we just walked past? Would you like a snack or a full meal? But the total context – the 'deep structure' – of the communication 'I am hungry' may never be known, even to the person who spoke the words. Who can say ultimately what amazingly vast network of associations may have given rise to that apparently simple and straightforward statement?

We realize from this that there are always 'hidden depths' to our thinking. However, the notion of the surface structure and deep structure of how and what we think and communicate leads to a number of immediately useful applications.

Preprocessing

We have already met this idea. It is related to the important principle of 'what we consciously attend to we subconsciously react to'. A seed thought is born in cognitive space and then forgotten – not lost, but allowed to drift down into the creative subconscious where it grows into a more complex structure. Later when we remind ourselves of the idea we often find we have more to say about it. Pedagogically we can make use of this by mentioning areas of work to our students ahead of time. If I'm starting a topic on, say, dinosaurs on Monday then I'll tell my class about that on the previous Friday. Throughout the weekend the students will be preprocessing 'dinosaurs', subconsciously gathering up scraps and fragments, ideas and associations from the subconscious map that link to the central concept. The Accelerated Learning Cycle encourages us to 'connect the learning'. This strategy becomes even more powerful when we encourage preprocessing in the students' own minds.

The meaning of any communication is the response it evokes

This is an important principle in the field of communication known as NLP (Neuro-Linguistic Programming) – which itself embodies the powerful realization that language affects (programs) mental, emotional and physical behaviour. 'Communication' here means the total context of the interaction, and so includes language, environment and the conscious and subconscious agendas of the communicators.

Even to begin to outline the strategies of NLP is beyond the scope of this section but even touching on the topic alerts us as educators to be more aware of 'communication contexts'. For example, run a brief communication audit to check the balance between

- teacher talk and class discussion
- students sitting and listening and students discussing
- teacher-initiated questions and student-initiated questions
- closed questions and open questions
- students being told and students finding out for themselves
- students giving (and teachers expecting) 'right answers' and students problem solving
- students copying (in whatever form) and students inventing
- worksheet exercises and 'real life' problems to be solved.

Increasing 'nosiness' about the classroom context of communication can quickly raise our awareness of other aspects of the language of schooling. Consider the following:

- That door has been left open.
- It simply isn't good enough.
- Hard work leads to greater achievement.
- As a dyslexic student he finds schoolwork harder.
- I should try to get better grades.
- He's always in trouble over homework assignments.

By simply adopting the attitude of nosiness we realize that all of the sentences beg questions, which reflect our impulse to 'contextualize', to learn more of the deeper structure supporting the surface structure of the words themselves.

- Who left the door open? For what possible reasons?
- What simply isn't good enough and in what ways? And why? And what might be good enough and why?

- What do you mean by 'hard'? Why should it be hard? How do you define 'achievement'? Whose definition of achievement are you using? Why?

- What do you mean by 'dyslexic'? (This particular term can be especially limiting. Notice how the sentence 'labels' the student. In NLP terminology this is a nominalization. I think of it as a 'name-inalization'. Such a label creates a state of being. The word 'state' in this sense is related to 'static', something that is 'still' or 'stuck'. It establishes what has been called a *hardening of the categories*, in other words, a mindset – by which I mean 'a mind, set'.)

- What stops you from trying? ('Should' usually indicates a hidden 'but'.) What ways of trying can you think of? How might they help you?

- Always? What kind of trouble? Why 'trouble'?

The simple act of noticing, and encouraging students to notice, what is limiting and liberating in their language can immediately enrich and empower classroom communication. Benjamin Bloom's 'taxonomy of thinking' model of learning postulates a hierarchy of thinking strategies that lead from simple thinking and little understanding to advanced thinking and fuller understanding.[9] I can't help but regard 'understanding' as 'that which is under us as we stand'. In other words, the platform of memory and experience and how our students use it that supports them as they are 'reared up' to be confident and independent creative thinkers.

The metaphor game and Velcro thinking

Language is entirely representational. 'The word is not the thing' is how this wisdom is often expressed. Playing with words and concepts through metaphorical thinking offers endless possibilities for greater learning and understanding to occur.

The metaphor game may take many forms. In every case the aim is to look at something in another way (as another 'thing') so that further insights are generated. Here are a few examples of what I mean:

- Mind metaphors

  The mind is a butterfly because ...?

  The mind is a spider web because ...?

  The mind is a rocketship because ...?

- Language metaphors

  Words are a river ... (because?)

  Language is a forest ...

  Insults are springs ...

  Jokes are flowers ...

Questions are fire …

Questions are water …

Books are mountains …

- Problem metaphors

  Wall problems are like this …

  Mirror problems are like this …

  Kitten problems are like this …

- Solution metaphors

  Wall solutions are like this …

  Snowfall solutions are like this …

  Pizza solutions are like this …

'Velcro thinking' is simply an extension of the metaphor idea. 'Thinking' is such an amazingly abstract and subtle concept that it's quite natural to want to 'get more of a handle on it' through the use of metaphors. We've already used the notion of thinking 'tools' and questions as 'instruments', but if thinking were like Velcro, how would it work? What would its strengths and weaknesses be? When might be useful times to apply Velcro thinking? And what about 'allotment thinking', 'barbecue thinking', 'binocular thinking'? The list is endless, which is an idea congruent with the mind's own infinite capacity to be creative.

Before leaving metaphors, you might find it fruitful to consider the metaphors embedded in the language of education itself. What messages, I wonder, do such metaphors communicate to our students? And what more helpful metaphors might we now want to employ?

- deliver
- targets
- levels
- exercises
- bright/dull
- fast/slow
- struggles
- catch up
- slip back

27

Quality questioning

The primary purpose of questioning is to generate more ideas and information, and it is one of the key elements of the creative attitude. A basic 'quality questioning' strategy is this three-step process:

1   What do I know?

2   What do I think I know?

3   What do I now need to find out?

The first question highlights the early state of 'knowingness' and represents surface structure: bare facts, initial observations and so on. The second question encourages exploration of the deeper structure of the context by recognizing assumptions and inferences, opinions, ambiguities, contradictions and so on. The third question focuses attention on further thinking/questioning strategies to elicit more information leading towards solutions.

The What-do-I-know Three-Step is often a useful starting point for any enquiry-based activity. Once students begin to differentiate the various kinds of questions that arise from it, and once they begin to actively initiate those questioning strategies for themselves (rather than being passive recipients of information or always prompted by teacher-led questions), then they will know what 'quality questioning' involves.

One broad distinction is that which exists between scientifically oriented questions and philosophically oriented questions. These are generic terms and don't just refer to questions arising within the fields of science and philosophy. Scientific type questions presuppose definite answers existing 'out there' that can be investigated through observation, experiment and other evidence-gathering procedures. The strategy for answering such questions is GAS – Go And See. Get out there and investigate! Philosophic questions don't presuppose definite answers (though they don't deny their existence) and realize that some questions may only lead to further questions. Here the emphasis is much more on themes and relationships, contexts and meanings. The usual strategy for exploring such questions is SATT – Sit And Think/Talk. Both kinds of questioning domains have their roots in NC – Natural Curiosity – and endeavour to learn more about the deep structure of human existence and experience.

A more detailed breakdown of question types is illustrated in Fig.1.2. Small/concrete/closed questions aim to elicit specific details – 'Are we having burgers or kebabs for supper?' (oh all right, salad if you prefer) or 'What is the time?'. These kinds of questions are convergent and point towards definite endpoints. Large/abstract/open questions aim to create overviews and unfold greater contexts. They tend to be more philosophic in nature and generate further questions – 'Why do some foods taste better than others?' or

'What is time?'. These questions are divergent and endpoints are often not an immediate feature.

Large and small questions:

Fig 1.2

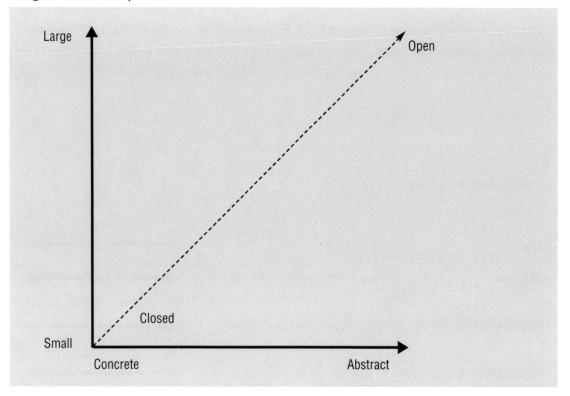

Fig. 1.3 offers a more detailed matrix for framing questions. Students may use some or all of the parameters to help decide what kind of question is most useful in any given situation. However, one of the most powerful motivators for students to learn and use quality questioning strategies is if we as educators display the creative attitude ourselves and build such questioning into our own behaviour. A wise old saying has it that a good teacher is never afraid to say 'I don't know, but how might we find out?'. If we vest our authority in how many facts or 'right answers' we know (or think we know) then our students' ability to learn how to learn will be inhibited. If we are comfortable with ambiguity, uncertainty and mystery – but remain enthusiastic to discover more – then our students will be encouraged to mimic our approach.

Incidentally, the word 'encourage' suggests 'giving courage to'. We can give courage to our students to question and express themselves by asking things like

- I'm interested in your idea. How did you reach that conclusion?
- How else could we explore/investigate/solve this problem?
- What other conclusions might be possible?

- How will you/we decide how to proceed?

- How can we develop this idea/argument, and so on?

- What other questions can we ask?

Finally, as an experiment, consider what could happen if you walked into the classroom one day and proclaimed 'This is the last statement I will make this lesson and will only speak to you using questions from now on! What would you like to say?'

Be assured of an interesting session!

Fig 1.3 Quality questions matrix:

		1 2 3 4 5 6
Scale	How big is this question?	← →
Openness	How many answers might this question lead to?	← →
Scientific / Technical	How surely can I investigate the right answer?	← →
Philosophical	How far can we only sit and think about possible answers?	← →
Relevance	How useful is this question?	← →
Depth	How much information might I gain?	← →
Flexibility	How many ways can I use the answer?	← →
Incisiveness	How many other questions might come from the answer?	← →
Subjectivity	How far is the answer someone's opinion?	← →
Learning Value	How much does the answer help my understanding?	← →
Insight	How far does the answer feel right to me?	← →
Divergence	How many other ideas might spring from the answer?	← →
Challenge	How deeply does the answer lead me to question, doubt and test my beliefs?	← →

Notes

1   See also www.sbowkett.freeserve.co.uk.

2   Abbott and Ryan (2000): they seem to be quoting Howard Gardner here in making the point (p. 21) that 'real understanding means overcoming personally held naive theories'.

3   In referring to this I went to Wilson and Grant, *The Directory of Possibilities* (1981). Wilson draws great inspiration from the work of the philosopher Arthur Koestler, whose massive *Act of Creation* (1965) is seminal.

4   Many books on creativity refer to Poincaré's ideas, for example, Evens and Deehan (1990), who also say many cogent things about the subconscious (referred to in their book as the Unconscious, after Freud).

5   The link between frequency of electrical impulses produced during brain activity and mental/physical states is well researched and widely reported. Cogent points are made for instance by Susan Greenfield in *The Human Brain* (1997).

6   Anchoring is a technique deriving from Neuro-Linguistic Programming (NLP), and has a wide range of applications. See O'Connor and Seymour (1990).

7   For more detail about the mechanisms of this process, see Guy Claxton's *Hare Brain, Tortoise Mind* (1998), which is significantly subtitled 'Why intelligence increases when you think less'!

8   Lewis and Pucelik (1993): this is a readable and very through presentation of the NLP 'take' on the surface and deep structure of language and communication.

9   Bloom's taxonomy is widely referenced. A useful summary within the context of thinking skills in the classroom is given by Rockett and Percival (2002).

31

A matter of fact

Trisha Lee

For as long as anyone could remember people had wanted Facts: fixed, actual, concrete truth. Finding the Facts became as important as breathing. No rock was left unturned in the search for Fact. Fact Seekers spent vast sums of government grants in the belief that one day they would reach their goal and all the Facts would be uncovered. When the first Fact was found, a strange Fact, a small see-through creature, it became an oracle to the Fact Seekers. A question of Fact was asked every day until the people discovered the whereabouts of the rest of the Fact family and made preparations for them to visit.

When they finally arrived one winter's morning – a sea of black and white Facts crawling out from the stones where they had been hiding – it was no surprise that the people welcomed them with open arms; embraced the Facts, ran out of their houses and drowned in a sea of Facts.

The Fact Seekers became National Heroes, and their role was changed from Fact Seeker to Fact Keeper. The Facts grew in power and stature, small Facts linking with bigger Facts to become tougher, stronger, concrete. As time went on, Useless Facts, Weird Facts, Amusing Facts, the undesirable cousins of the Fact Family, began to grow up, and as they grew they became Hard Facts. Laws changed so only these Facts remained. The children who were alive at the time of the arrivals also grew up, becoming adults After the Fact; they got married, had children of their own and time ticked on.

That was all long ago, so long ago that few people could remember what it was like Before the Fact. Those who had memories of that time either kept it to themselves for fear that it would disprove the Fact or they visited the Fact Keepers, where they gave up all of their memories in exchange for all of the Facts. And all this seemed perfectly normal to them, normal, that is, until a strange occurrence.

It began at Shelter 1, Truthful Way; the home of the first true generation of Fact Dwellers. It started with Alethea. On a Tuesday morning. The morning she couldn't speak.

Alethea's voice caught in her throat and stayed there, a ball of fire unable to free itself from the volcano of her mouth.

The doctor was called. Alethea opened wide, allowed the cold metal instrument to peer inside, see all the frustration that welled up in her, and then watched in surprise as it withdrew. Heads shook. The doctor hadn't noticed, hadn't seen her voice sitting there at the corner of her mind. She tried to communicate to him through the language of her silence, but was greeted by the back of his head, retreating footsteps and a closed door.

The doctor said there was no reason for it. No Fact could be given as to why it was happening. Nothing could cause this silence to come into existence and therefore it didn't exist and if it didn't exist then neither did Alethea. That became Fact; everyone around her was made to see this Fact. Alethea vanished.

The Fact Keepers took her. Locked her in a place with white walls and cold sheets, a world where colour was extinct. She had become a Matter of Fact.

But the problem came back. Later that same week, more doctors were called to other shelters. Voices, unable to be heard, screeched out in silence, begging for someone to see where their retreating words were hiding. The place with the white walls and the cold sheets began to fill – and yet, for all of its busyness, its crowded beds, it was the quietest place on earth.

Nobody spoke about the Silent Ones. The Fact was they didn't exist, not in this world. As neighbours, friends, daughters or sons vanished away, they were replaced by Facts that proved that they never existed. Nobody but the Fact Keepers could question a Fact.

Verity knew it was wrong to question but something didn't feel right anymore. For several days now she had been having memories of a Silent One. Somewhere in the back of her mind she could picture her daughter, brown-eyed, staring out from behind long dark lashes, eyes that spoke, pleaded, beseeched. She tried hard to wipe the thoughts from her mind.

Her daughter stolen away in the middle of the night; a doctor in a white coat, words shouted at her. "If the silence doesn't exist then neither does Alethea." Fact Keepers playing with her mind, distorting her memory. But no! It could not be true. There was no proof and without proof it could not be Fact. So why was she haunted by these images?

That night before she went to sleep she visited the Fact Keeper, asked about her daughter, was reassured that such contemplations were not Facts and as the electronic pulse was placed to her forehead all thoughts of a child vanished.

As the lights turned off in the room with the white walls and the cold sheets, the Silent Ones stirred. During the night the observations were less intrusive and if they were careful, took it in turns to listen at the door and watch for the Fact Keepers, then sometimes, if they were really lucky, they could Gather.

As the lights turned off in Verity's room she found herself falling into a deep sleep. The electronic pulse was still beating in time with her heart and sleep welcomed her into its dark fold.

For the Silent Ones the Gathering was beginning.

Brown eyes, long dark lashes, calling out to Verity from the darkness. An electronic pulse, pushing and pulsating against her heart, covering up the dark lashes and the brown eyes with its persistent beat.

The Silent Ones stare at each other from across the Gathering, think of what they have left behind, picture faces, names and places with only their eyes to speak for them. Alethea is strong. She was the first to arrive and the memory of her mother's face and her mother's voice runs out of her, out through her eyes, down through her fingers and into the room for the others to feel.

Verity thrashes in her sleep, fighting with the Facts. Suddenly Alethea is besides her, helping her fight. The Facts rise up against the pair. Mother and daughter united in battle.

"Imagine, invent, create," Alethea laughs out to her mother.

"I don't know how to," sighs Verity.

"Copy me," her daughter directs, and closes her eyes for the briefest of seconds. A flash of light appears in the dream world and a bolt of lightning knocks over the Hard Fact in front of them. The Fact falls apart, lies motionless on the ground for a while, then realizes that the lightning does not really exist. Content that if this is the case, then it is unhurt, the Fact rises to join the rest of its family and continues to march forward towards Alethea and her mother.

"Imagine a brick wall between them and us," Alethea shouts. Immediately a brick wall is created that runs from one end of Verity's mind to the other, shutting out the Facts.

"There's no colour in here," laughs Alethea, closing her eyes again, and within seconds the earth becomes covered in dark green grass. A forest rises up from the ground, reaching out to the clear blue sky. A sun is born, bright yellow at first, and then turning red, purple, orange. A stream appears, fishes swimming, jumping, humming, flying. A bird, clad in feathers of red and gold, flies towards the sun. As it nears its destination the mournful lament of its song can be heard echoing across the world. Suddenly the bird explodes into flame and its ashes fall to the ground. Then, before the ashes have had time to disperse on the wind, a new bird is formed, sings a song of life and flies out towards the forest.

The sound of Facts crashing into a brick wall suddenly breaks through the song of the Phoenix. Bang! Splat! Crash!

"If the wall doesn't exist then we can't be hurting ourselves on it," says the voice of a Hard Fact.

The wall vanishes. But Verity's mind has opened now and it is not only Alethea who is capable of bringing imaginings into existence. Keen to try out her new powers Verity looks at the black and white Fact approaching her and imagines a zebra dancing in the jungle of her mind. Whatever she wishes for appears, the more original her thoughts the more inventive her creations.

They stand before the Facts, mother and daughter, armed only with their imaginings, and the Facts can't stop them. Shaken by uncertainty, weakened by fiction, the Facts make a hasty retreat.

"Run after the Facts!" screams Verity, excited by the newness of her mind. But Alethea stops her.

"We have been chasing the Facts for so long that we lost sight of the fiction. Enjoy the magic of this world for a while longer. There is far more here for you to discover."

Verity hugs her daughter and deep in her mind she can hear the imaginings of all the Silent Ones, neighbours and friends from long ago, who she had forgotten existed, singing and dreaming, chatting and whispering in a world where anything can happen.

As tiredness reaches her, the light of the sun fades and she lies for a while in her daughter's arms, watching the stars, joining the dots with her finger till sleep welcomes her home.

The next day Verity awakes. She is back in her own room, back in the world of Fact. She tries hard to speak, but her voice is caught in her throat and stays there, a ball of fire unable to free itself from the volcano of her mouth.

Curiosity killed the cat

Trisha Lee

Curiosity; an eager desire to know or learn about something

Curiosity is the essence of creativity; a series of what ifs, questions without a known answer, the mother of invention.

From the moment we are born the learning skills that will support us through life are already in place: natural curiosity. Babies begin their exploration of how life works by putting things into their mouths, exploring the taste, texture and feel of an object. Young children are equally curious. As they grow they begin questioning, enquiring, searching, manipulating and experimenting and before they even enter school they are already engaged in one of the most creative activities at the heart of learning: play.

If a new object or experience is introduced to a group of young children, some of them will come forward immediately while others are more cautious – but all the children will, in their own time, need a closer look, and then a touch, a stroke, a hold, a feel. They act on natural curiosity and need a creative encounter with that object.

Does this need to explore, to have a creative encounter, to find out how things work or what makes something tick ever go away? When I work with a class of children and I ask for someone to volunteer I am always greeted by a forest of waving hands before the children even know what activity they will be involved in. When I sit in front of a group of adults during an INSET session and I ask for a volunteer I look around the room and watch as everyone shuffles, looks down, desperately tries to avoid eye contact and the room takes on an edge of nervous apprehension.

What is it that changes us from curious, eager to engage, creative three year olds into adults who are nervous about taking risks or being exposed? Maybe the expression 'curiosity killed the cat' does more than simply warn us about the hidden dangers in exploring the unknown and actually blocks us completely from taking those risks. How many of us were told we were no good at something when we were children and have taken that belief with us into our adult lives? Drawing, writing, singing? Maybe the story one of us created wasn't the story the teacher wanted. Maybe we were told off for playing with something, engaging in fantasy when we should have been learning facts. As we grow through education the cat is truly killed. We learn to hide the curiosity, ignore the creativity, put away the childish play and enter into the world of adulthood.

Child's play

'Child's play' – a phrase filled with connotations that play is anything but important: but take a moment to look more closely at children playing and it will soon become apparent that 'child's play' is a highly serious endeavour. Vivian Gussin Paley begins her book, *A Child's Work* (2004), by stating that 'play is the work of children'. Before a child can come to terms with reality, they must have some frame of reference to evaluate it. The tools they use for this are play, fantasy, curiosity and creativity. And yet, with the introduction of the National Curriculum in 1988 and the need for children to learn facts and for us to test and grade their knowledge of these, there also began to creep in the suppression of fantasy, the stifling of creativity, the killing of the cat.

There was an increasing emphasis on getting 'Back to basics'; but this metamorphosed into an approach that did not consider the basic tools that children need to understand and make sense of the world. Was the rigour of the three 'R's put back into the curriculum because children were unable to recite number facts and spell in the way as their forefathers had, forefathers who were now in power? Is the current swing towards creativity a result of adults who were children in the 1960s and 1970s placing an emphasis back on the topic-based approach they themselves received at school? And when do we find the time to listen to the voices of the children themselves?

Whatever the reasoning behind the National Curriculum's drive for a return to fact-based learning, the arrival of the facts definitely began to force creative thought to sneak away and hide. Many teachers became frightened of failing to meet targets and scoring badly for their schools in league tables and so became reluctant to take risks outside the strategies and methodology that the National Curriculum proposed.

The children of the 1980s might be better spellers than those of the 1960s and 1970s but when faced with a challenge to which there is no set answer, facts are of little use. It is our curiosity, the ability to prod and manipulate, explore, understand what factors are influencing a situation, what possibilities these throw up, how to have a creative encounter with the problem that bring forth the best solutions.

It is now being said that '60 per cent of the jobs primary school children will do when they leave school haven't been invented yet', and there is a dawning realization that being able to spell isn't going to create these jobs. What children need in the twenty-first century is a belief in the importance of their curiosity, their ability to invent fantasy solutions so that as they grow older they can develop these fantasies further and maybe make them real. When Jules Verne was engaged in writing did he have any idea that so many of his imaginings would become reality? Would any of the inventions of our time have come to light if people had concentrated only on the facts and not had the time to dream? It is our capacity for imagination that enables us to solve the problems posed by reality.

When we ask questions that we don't know the answers to, we engage with the world that children explore every day through their play. The highly creative pre-school child learns by taking risks, manipulating, testing and then modifying ideas. If we could incorporate this natural curiosity into our classrooms how much more engaging would our lessons be? Questions that have only a factual answer demand skills of memory and recall from a child. Questions that have 'what if's in their answer involve an understanding of the norm as well as a creative evaluation of what might be possible. To answer such a question we have to take a risk, test out our theories and gradually modify our ideas; we have to enter the world of fantasy play.

Every year at Christmas my mother would buy me a new watch. Much to her frustration, by Christmas night the watch was always in pieces. The fact that the watch would tell me the time was less interesting to me than what happened inside a watch to make the hands move. Needless to say my mother stopped buying me watches in the end, and to this day I still don't wear one. But these questions – How does it work? What do I need to do to make something else possible? What happens if I do this? – these are the questions children ask every day and try out through their play.

Kieran Egan, in *Primary Understanding* (1988) and *Teaching as Storytelling* (1989), proposes that you can teach anything through storytelling, even mathematics. By engaging children in explorations through fantasy we can cover any topic in a way that taps into the creative process that children use naturally to make sense of the world. A creative classroom puts children's play and creativity at the heart of its curriculum and concentrates on making lessons memorable experiences for every child. When the lesson is woven together through a good story children find a way to engage with it more easily. However, in order to make lessons more creative in this way we also have to change the way we think about teaching.

At present so much of teaching is geared around the teacher's story. The teacher's story is 'I have to teach maths, or grammar or history, I know what my class need to learn and my story is making sure I teach it to them'. But what is the child's story?

In Vivian Gussin Paley's kindergarten classroom in Chicago she placed the child's story at the heart of her curriculum. By developing a technique of storytelling and story acting she managed to engage all the children in an activity where they regularly dictated their stories. Paley would then scribe these stories verbatim, and at the end of each day she led the class in acting them out. This simple technique when used with a class of children from the age of three upwards has quite dramatic effects. I have worked successfully using this technique to scribe stories from children across the whole spectrum of abilities, including children for whom English is a second language, and even children who withdraw from any activity that involves working with an adult.

A girl who was an elective mute once whispered breathlessly to me her one-word story, the first word she had ever said within the classroom: 'Princess'. When she stepped onto the taped-out stage in the corner of the classroom to act out her story she engaged with the part wholeheartedly: this silent girl, now in role as the haughty princess, walking confidently around the stage surveying her kingdom. This is the power of storytelling and story acting.

When I run INSET sessions to introduce this approach to teachers I always start with a demonstration, working with a group of 15 children who I have never met before. As I sit cross-legged on the floor with the four or five year olds, encircled by 20 or more adults on chairs, there is always a moment of anxiety. But once I begin, telling a story that a child from another school has told to me, and asking the children to come up in turn around the stage to take part in acting out this story, I immediately relax. The children, within seconds of my starting, recognize the work. Acting out to them is familiar, the play that they are engaged in every day. As I ask the child next to me to come up and play the puppy in the story, all I am doing is repeating what children do in their play every day as they say to each other, 'You be the mum and I'll be the baby and the baby is crying.' When all the children have taken a turn at acting in a story I ask if any of them want to tell me a story. The 20 or more adults on chairs have by this time disappeared for both me and the children, and we are alone together in this room where anything is possible. I am surrounded by a sea of hands, and as the first child opens her mouth to begin the story she is greeted by silence from her peers. Nothing is more interesting to a child than the story of another.

'Once there was a baby bird …' and the story pours forth. I scribe each sentence, saying aloud the words I write as they tumble down from the child before me. When the story is finished the acting out begins. The children choose which character they would like to play in the story and the stage is soon filled with the enactment of scenes that mesmerize the watching audience, adults and children alike.

This to me is like a little piece of magic. The moment storytelling and story acting begins I am no longer a stranger in the classroom. In the same way as the new child in a group is often swallowed up quickly in play – 'What's your name? What's your name? Do you want to play?' – I have been absorbed into the classroom as the children and I work together bringing to life our stories. How wonderful the world would be if adults could welcome in strangers so easily. When adults meet in a new situation we may try to find out about each other by asking questions and engaging in discussion. If the same group of strangers were put together in a drama workshop, however, they might know less about each others' backgrounds and experiences by the end of an hour, but they are closer, having laughed, played games and acted out together. Such is the work of children, these are the tools that they have to break down barriers, and regrettably we place them at the bottom of the pile when it comes to tools for learning.

I was told a story by a four year old:

> Once there was a baby bird. It flew and flew until it found a shiny tree. 'Mum, Mum look, I seed a shiny tree, come and look.' 'There's no such thing as a shiny tree,' said the mum. The baby bird flew the mum to the shiny tree. 'Look, look there is a shiny tree.' And the mum saw the shiny tree and said, 'Let's pick all the shiny leaves off.'
>
> So they did.

I thought about this story for a long time afterwards. When the girl acted it out she took the role of the baby bird, desperately trying to persuade her mother to look at the shiny tree. The child playing the mother also understood the role. Folded arms, shaking head: 'There's no such thing as a shiny tree.' How often had these children been told that? How often do we as adults deny the shiny tree that our children try to show us? Or then, to make matters worse, when the children finally persuade us to reach the shiny tree, how often do we try to change it, pick the leaves off, and try to make it better rather than just marvelling at it for what it is?

Storytelling and story acting

A practical guide to the Helicopter Technique[1]

Trisha Lee

The Helicopter Technique recognizes the potential in even the youngest of children to undertake the serious role of telling, observing and acting out in the theatre of the classroom. It is a simple technique. The teacher or workshop leader sits down with the child, listens to his/her story, and writes it down word for word. At the end of the story, the child decides which character he/she wants to play and the teacher moves onto the next child on the list. Towards the end of the session, the whole class gathers to act out the stories of their peers.

The Helicopter Technique is suitable for children from the moment they start to talk. We have worked successfully with two and a half year olds, and the process really comes into its own with children from Nursery and Reception-age classrooms. The benefits of the technique are immense, particularly in relation to children's speaking and listening skills, confidence, language development and development of their knowledge of story and story form. Although this approach is relevant for pupils throughout primary school, it is of paramount benefit in Foundation Stage and Key Stage 1.

Why is it called the Helicopter Technique? One teacher who had been delivering the technique in her classroom for a number of sessions told me that she thought the reason behind the name came from the way we select children to be involved in the action. This is done by going around the stage, taking it in turns, and she related this motion to the blades of a helicopter turning around. Although I really like this idea, the name actually comes from the title of the book *The Boy Who Would be a Helicopter* by Vivian Gussin Paley (1991).

Vivian Gussin Paley is a now retired kindergarten teacher from the University of Chicago Laboratory School in the state of Illinois. She received a MacArthur Fellowship in 1989, an Erikson Award for Service to Children in 1987, and a Lifetime Achievement American Book Award from the Before Columbus Foundation in 1998. She is the author of many books describing her work with children who are just starting school. In 2002, Vivian Gussin Paley agreed to become patron to MakeBelieve Arts.

How to introduce the Helicopter Technique to a class

First: create a stage

Using masking tape, mark out a rectangle on the classroom floor that will act as your stage. It is impossible to give an approximate measurement for this; the most important thing is that all the children should be able to sit around the outside of the stage and for there to be enough room for them all to have front row seats. As soon as the stage is down ask the children to sit around the edges, spreading themselves out over all four sides.

> **Rule**   Children should not enter the marked-out stage area unless they are involved in the story acting.

Although the above rule is there for a reason, there are times when it can and should be broken. Some young children have problems sitting for long periods, or find it impossible not to crawl onto the stage. Adults are often not as tolerant of this as children. Remember that a teacher who continually tries to get one child off the stage could break the trust and focus of the whole activity. Try to understand the child's needs and do not let story acting become something a teacher feels they have to control. It is a step up from play and as such has a more chaotic sense of rules attached. On the other hand, do take time to establish a culture of listening within the classroom

43

Second: involve the class in acting out stories from other children

Once the class are settled around the stage begin by introducing them to two or three stories that you have either created yourself or been told by other children. Here is a scripted prompt that may help you to introduce the technique:

> Today we are going to do some story acting. The first stories I am going to use come from another school, a long way away in America.[2] The children in that school told stories to their teacher and here is one of them for us to act out.
> *A little puppy saw a flower.*
> In fact, let's start there. Can you play the puppy? Will you come up onto the stage? How does the puppy walk? Can you show me? And you, will you come up and be the flower. Can you pretend to be the flower? Can you show me how it will look?
> *The puppy smelt the flower.*
> Can I see you smell the flower?
> *And he saw a tree.*
> Will you come and be the tree? How can you show me that you are a tree? Fantastic!
> *The puppy walked all the way around the tree, until his mother came to find him.*
> Would you be the mother dog coming to find him? How does the mother dog walk?
> And that is the end of the story. Let's all clap thank you to the story actors?

It is always advisable to use at least two or three stories to introduce the technique. In this way all the children find out what is involved in acting out a story before they begin to tell stories of their own. (There are several story examples in Figures 1 and 2 at the end of the chapter 'Peer group education' that could be adapted for this purpose.) Make sure that every child is offered the chance to get on the stage and become a character or object in at least one of these stories. (If you have a large class of children you may need to use four or five stories in your introduction, or be imaginative with the number of trees or tigers in a story, and so on.) This way all the children will have had the

chance to see what story acting involves and be able to participate in the activity in their own way.

Rule   No child should ever be forced, coerced or made to feel obliged to act out in a story or to tell a story.

Finally: collect stories from one or two of the children as they sit around the stage...

Having acted out a few stories, the children are now in a position to move onto telling their own stories. When introducing the technique for the first time collect one or two stories from children as they are seated around the stage. The advantage to this is that all the children can see, at first hand, exactly what happens when they tell a story. As you collect each story, act it out immediately, asking the author which character he/she wants to play and casting the rest of the characters from children in their places around the stage.

The main points for scribing stories are as follows:

● Write the children's stories word for word as they are dictated.

● Repeat aloud the words of the child whose story you are scribing as you write.

● Show the children around the stage that you are writing down their words.

● NB: first stories, dictated in a large group, are often short and nervously told.

Once you have run an introductory session of about 20 minutes with a group of children they will be confident of all aspects of the work and eager to tell their own stories. You are then ready to set up a regular storytelling and story acting timeslot and introduce it into your weekly plan.

Private storytelling

If you ask whether a child wants to tell a story and he/she says no or shakes his/her head, validate the decision, with a phrase like 'No, you just want to listen? Good, we need story listeners too'.

The storybook

The format the teacher decides on to keep the stories is really down to the individual. A special book may initially give a feeling of prestige to the children's words. Some of our workshop leaders have used beautiful books to show the value they place on the stories collected. After a while though, we became aware that this was more for ourselves than for the children, who were equally as happy to dictate onto scraps of paper. We show the children that we value them through writing their stories down and acting them out. Some teachers type up the stories, and put them in children's records to show the progression of a child. This can become a laborious task and it would be a tragedy if this exercise made storytelling/story acting seem like a chore.

In recent years, MakeBelieve Arts have discovered duplicate books, which are not only really useful for keeping a record of the stories for ourselves but also enable us to hand over a copy of the stories that we have collected to the class teacher at the end of each session.

The book or paper used can be either A4 or A5 in size. If A4, it is advisable to write with double line spacing and in large handwriting. If A5, there is less need to really space out the lines, but judge this for yourself, depending on the size of your handwriting. If the stories are too long they can become difficult and time consuming to act out.

Rule   Storytelling is a communal activity.

Do not worry about other children joining in, or commenting during the dictation of another child's story. The author has the absolute right to accept or reject the suggestions offered by his/her peers.

Our kind of storytelling is a social phenomenon, intended to flow through all other activities and provide the widest opportunity for a communal response. (Paley, 1990)

Beginning dictation

The hardest thing about scribing a story is learning to really listen to the words of young children. As adults, we may think we listen but often we hear things in the way we would understand them, which is not always in the way they are meant. Often as adults we interrupt or try to steer or guide children, asking them questions to pin them down. If a child mentions a star, we may think that it is in the child's best interest to be prompted to describe the star. Often what this does is make the child think they are wrong and their star, so clearly seen in their eyes, begins to lose its worth. There is a time and a place for developing adverbs, but story dictation is not one of these. The teacher's role in story dictation is to listen, write down word for word what the child dictates, and only ask questions to clarify points that they do not understand.

Do not be afraid to interrupt the child whose sentences never end or who never stops for breath. S/he will stop when you begin repeating the words as you scribe and you will begin to set a pace at which you can write. Remind the child that you can't write as fast as s/he speaks and invite him or her to help make sure that you have written everything exactly as s/he wants it.

Rule   Each story should take no more than one page.

As children get more familiar with the technique, their stories will get longer. The one page per story rule means that all children's stories get the chance to be acted out on the day they are taken down. It is important to remember that stories can also be very short. One word can be a story, as can a whole page. If a child is telling a longer story than the one page rule allows, suggest to them that at the next story dictation session they continue their story, as another chapter in a long book.

As the child dictates to you, repeat every word, word for word, setting the pace of your own writing. As you write 'the', say 'the', as you write 'dog', say 'dog', and so on. Let the child dictate a whole sentence before you begin scribing (or as many words as you can remember). This will make sure that you do not break down the pace of the story into individual words and hamper the flow for the child. As you and the children grow more confident you will find the ideal pace for them and yourself so that you capture everything.

'And then what happens?'

As a reserve question for a child who is struggling, this phrase may offer a guiding hand. Be careful not to ask it too much though, as you may find yourself falling into the trap of asking it after every sentence and then cutting the child off when they come to the end of the page. This question also demands an action, which if overused, can result in your leading the child on the sentence structure.

'Is there any more to your story?'

This is a less judgemental question than 'And then what happens?' or 'Is that the end?'. It sends a message to the child that their story is in their control. Remember that one word, or a short sentence, can be a story. As children's language and storytelling techniques develop, they will begin to add more words.

When the story is complete

When the child has finished dictating a story, take a moment to run through the characters with them and then ask which character they would like to play when their story is acted out. Underline all the characters in the story as you read through it and finally circle the one the child decides to represent. Some children may choose to just watch their story acted out. This is fine; sometimes we just want to see others play out our stories.

Number of characters

After the storyteller has decided on their character, take a few minutes to clear up any confusion you have with the narrative. If the story contains baddies, find out how many baddies there are in the story. If the child says a very high number, use this time to negotiate, being realistic about how many baddies will fit on the stage.

Children who will not speak

When a child comes willingly to the story table but then sits staring at you without speaking, it is sometimes hard to know what to do. Often the child wants to be involved in the activity, but lacks the confidence to speak, sitting on the chair in front of you being the first big step for him/her.

The rule of not leading a child can be broken in these situations, but needs to be done sensitively. Rather than listening to the child, the scribe relies on watching the child and asking the child questions based on their actions.

Watch the child's movements – if there are objects on the table they will probably be playing with them, so use these as a prompt to help the child.

> Is there a …(for example, lion)… in your story?

If this gets a nod, then watch the child move the animal or object. Say what you see.

> The lion walked. Walk, walk, walk, the lion stopped… and so on.

The story can be short. Ask the child regularly if they want you to write down what has been said, and continue through the same story dictation process as above. Sometimes this will not work, and if after a while nothing is happening, ask the child if they would like to tell you a story another day. Sometimes once a child sits on the chair, they feel trapped and need your permission to leave. If this is the case they will run off immediately you say this and you will know that this time they just wanted to try sitting on the chair – next time maybe they will tell you a story.

In one Nursery class I worked with a girl who spoke very little English. She sat by me every time I opened my storybook and then she held my hand and led me to the area of the room where the objects she needed to tell her story were placed. I remember one day I was sitting in front of a box of dinosaurs while she pointed and mimed until her story was finished. If I got the word wrong, like for example when I said 'the dinosaurs fought' when she wanted me to write 'the dinosaurs went raaaaaah', she shook her head, and continued to mime and point till her story was exactly the way she wanted it. Although taking a story from her was often hard work and I had to really concentrate, the joy that she greeted the completed version with made it worthwhile.

Story acting

When acting out the stories, ensure it is in an area where all the children have room to sit comfortably in a circle, and that there is enough room in the middle, for the marked-out stage area.

Allow at least 15 to 20 minutes for story acting, which should enable you to act out at least seven to eight stories, building on this as you and your class become more confident. Be sure to make story acting a fast-paced activity in your classroom.

Rule   All children should be present for the acting out.

Read the first sentence of the story. Then moving clockwise around the group, cast children to play the various roles contained in that sentence. Remember that the character the author is playing has been decided on by them and circled during story dictation.

Once the first characters are on stage, read the next line and bring in more actors. Make sure you pace the reading of the story to allow space for the children to respond to the narrative.

Rule   Do not force acting – this will come eventually.

Ask questions that will prompt the storyteller, or other children, to demonstrate their actions.

'I am curious to know how the lion moves – could you show me?'

The role of the storyteller

The storyteller, or author, is the creator of the narrative. Consult them on how a character might move, or a house might stand. If another child is hesitant, ask the storyteller to demonstrate the required actions.

What game are the children playing?

Asking children to be specific in their actions helps with the acting out of the story. Following for example a sentence 'the children are playing', find out during story acting exactly what the children are playing. Always ask the storyteller first – if they remain silent then ask the other children. When they respond, take this immediately back to the storyteller. Are the children playing ball? If s/he nods then accept the offer; if the child disagrees, by this stage s/he will be much more likely to say what game the children are playing.

Vivian Paley wrote in 1986:

> Place this three year old in a room with other threes, and sooner or later they will become an acting company. Should there happen to be a number of somewhat older peers about to offer stage directions and dialogue, the metamorphosis will come sooner rather than later.

> The dramatic images that flutter through their minds as so many unbound streams of consciousness novels, begin to emerge as audible scripts to be performed on demand.

49

Thanking

At the end of each story, remind the children to clap thank you to the storyteller and the story actors. This helps to reinforce the role of the audience and shows appreciation for sharing the work.

Additional points
Choosing

The storyteller *does not* have the power to cast his/her play.

> **Rule**   *Never* let the storyteller choose the children who act in their story. Take children from their place around the stage.

To allow this choice is to make story acting an activity that some children may never have the chance to experience. Children will incorporate friends in their stories and those that do not fit into these groups will become excluded.

Remember this technique is one step up from play. Play is a flexible tool, which children are used to negotiating and controlling. To help children facilitate these negotiations is highly valuable, but do not try to stop these negotiations taking place.

Cliché actions

By the time we become adults, we have acquired a selection of standard movements to demonstrate actions. If someone asks us to cook, we may imagine a saucepan and begin to stir; throwing a ball may consist of an over-arm throw. When working with children, it is easy to demonstrate an action, but if we keep still, the unaided actions that children come up with are often surprising and far more interesting.

If you catch yourself demonstrating, and realize it is a habit you find hard to break, sit on your hands during story acting and watch what the children do without your help. Monitor the difference between this and what they do when you demonstrate.

People as objects

Some objects can be mimed, or made out of children's bodies. If a story contains a castle, ask the child if they want someone to play the castle. Then ask them how the castle stands. Do not clutter the story with objects but if there is something that grabs your imagination or feels important in the story, then suggest that someone plays it.

> **Rule**   Remember not to impose your own way of creating object shapes on the children. Let them solve the problem themselves.

Sound effects

If a child's story has any elements that inspire sound effects, then enjoy working with the whole class to create these. If a wind is blowing ask the storyteller what the wind sounds like, and then involve the audience in creating this.

Stories with dialogue

Where a character has a line of dialogue, ask the child playing the character to say the line. If a child is reluctant to speak, try getting the whole class to say the words together. If the story suggests dialogue, ask the storyteller if the character says anything. This may prompt a line or phrase.

Less confident children

If a child wants to be involved in the action, but obviously lacks confidence, ask the storyteller if you can have two people taking that role. Most children will feel more confident to get on the stage when they have the person sitting next to them playing alongside them.

Story content

Often children will repeat images, or whole stories, dictated by their peers. This may seem disconcerting but is a result of their interest and enjoyment. It's good to positively acknowledge this:

'Sandy must have really liked your story – look, she has included a magic garden too.'

The Helicopter Technique of Storytelling and Story Acting places creativity at the centre of learning and gives a valuable insight into how individual children see the world. When practised regularly, it is hard not to be inspired by the wealth of images conjured up by each child and to listen in awe as they take on the important roles of actor, narrator, director, where every member is valued for what they are able to contribute and where their stories create the vibrant theatre of the classroom.

Approach this work with curiosity and enjoyment.

Notes

1 Adapted from the *Helicopter Technique Teachers Resource Pack* by Trisha Lee, MakeBelieve Arts, The Deptford Mission, 1 Creek Road, Deptford, London SE8 3BT, www.makebelievearts.co.uk

2 Vivian Gussin Paley stories, dictated during the making of the video, 'The Child Who Could Tell Stories', Ball State University, Indianapolis, October 2000.

Dialogue with the past

Roy Leighton

Stella, petite, determined and in a floral dress that echoed the vibrant colours of the landscape, stomped through fields turning golden with the advent of harvest. She was oblivious to the rampant beauty of her native Greece. Fury prevented her from seeing the magnificent landscape of the small coastal village she had been born and raised in. Her thin, attractive, olive-skinned, make-up-free face was creased with rage.

Anger and frustration were not uncommon for Stella. She had been born defensive, and seemed even as a child to find criticism difficult to accept. Anyone too dogmatic she found hard to tolerate. Her father was caring, intelligent and opinionated. Her loathing for his strong opinions often clouded her awareness of his concern and love. As soon as she was able she had moved from the village, and her visits became less frequent. She had returned this year to attend her mother's funeral, and to sell the house that had been in her family for generations. A combination of complex and slow-moving bureaucracy meant a stay that should only have been a matter of weeks was now moving into its sixth month. With no children, and with supportive business partners and a semi-retired husband, this shift was at least possible, if not without complications.

The paperwork, the sheaves of documents for the disposal of her family home – was now all ready for signing. Once this final duty had been completed she could shake off the dust of this place, return to her home in England and never again have an excuse or reason to return.

It was this that had sparked off an argument with her husband which had been bubbling for the past few weeks and come to a head moments earlier. He had attempted to discuss the possibility of keeping the property and moving there, or at least keeping it as a second home. She had dismissed his suggestions, but he had insisted that she listen to the argument and she had been equally determined to have her say. The usual approach. The usual outcome. He gets louder, she accuses him of shouting her down and storms out. She could not convey all the reasons for her ambivalence; she wasn't clear in her own mind. It was easier to resort to past habits of argument than to adopt a new approach of listening and discussing.

Spurred on by her fury, she headed for the solitary old olive tree in the field beyond her home.

The 'Old Man' had been growing there for hundreds of years, and was her sanctuary and place of calm reassurance. It had come by its name due to the twisted trunk and arching branches that in shadow created the silhouette of an old man – bent, arms open and beckoning. When the wind blew, as it did well and often, the 'Old Man's bowing and bending made it appear to nod, as if talking or listening intently to another.

Since her childhood several decades ago she had been drawn to the craggy, twisted tree. Its location on the side of the hill overlooking the coastal village was stunning. The seasons vied with one another to attack the senses with varying degrees of intensity.

Spring brought the aching possibility of new life, in the buds and in the calamitous chirping and swooping of oystercatchers, black-winged stilts and numerous other birds returning from migration. From spring, the life around the tree would move into the swooning heat and dazzling haze of summer, when the sun's intensity made the ground dance and distorted time. Autumn allowed a cooling in the heat and an explosion of colour, as flowers burst forth to celebrate their magnificence. With the winter's cold, although snow seldom visited, the sky and sea, and even the land, changed to a darker and harder blue. Silence and reflection were demanded by the winter landscape, and the people took their signal and moved more slowly and thought deeply.

And all the time the wind blew. No season was without the wind that whipped the sea, sending waves arching and frothing onto the rocks that jutted from the cliff face, defying both wind and sea.

54

The island was on the cusp between spring and summer when Stella advanced with single-minded determination towards the tree, and it was late in the afternoon when she arrived there. The twenty-minute walk had not lessened her fury, resentment and pace, and she stopped with a jolt, placing her hand on the gnarled trunk and falling into the tree's cool shade. Its touch and shelter and smell calmed her and she crumpled onto the small shady patch of grass and pink-headed *Matthiola triscupidata* flowers, known locally as 'Sad stock'. Her frustration was still evident but her anger had transmuted into a mixture of bewilderment and sadness, and the kind of loneliness that only occurs when two people who are sometimes very close have become, if only for a moment, very far apart.

"Just once! Just once!" she repeated. "If he could do it just once, then there would be something. Something there. Something to show that it was all worth it. Something to, to–" Her voice trailed off. Her head slumped into her palms and, as if this was a signal, her whole body appeared to wilt.

"What kind of something are you hoping for and how will you know it when it arrives?"

For a moment Stella was not sure if the voice was coming from within her own head or outside it.

Silence.

"I said 'What kind of something are you hoping for and how will you know it when it arrives?'"

Silence.

The voice was low, resonant and calm. It was instantly reassuring and direct. The kind of voice that does not waste words, time or silence. It belonged either to an old but still physically and mentally active man or to the tree. Stella's logical mind disregarded the momentary, whimsical idea that the tree was speaking and she answered, in a voice more angry than she intended, "Who wants to know?"

Silence.

"I think we are both curious to find out."

The voice this time approached nearer, and in front of Stella, from his earlier resting place under the tree now between her and the sea, stood Socrates. Not the Socrates who established his school of philosophy in this very region some two thousand years before. That would be too fantastical, unbelievable and impossible to accept for a mind so driven by modern psychological thought.

No, this Socrates was the retired village schoolteacher, who now occasionally took visitors on excursions to discover local history and culture. He was an expert on the life and work of his namesake and took a quiet pride both in the knowledge that he had studied and applied and also in sharing the same name.

He remembered Stella from her schooldays, when she was a bright and articulate girl with few friends and an active mind. He had been there through her adolescence when everything about the village where she lived seemed to aggravate and annoy her. He was there when she left at eighteen to study psychology and politics in Athens and had watched her return six months ago with her husband (some forthright English academic type who spoke only when he had to and never spoke Greek at all). This was the first time they had met since her return and he was grateful of the chance to welcome her back. He felt that now was the right time, not only to meet but also to talk.

"What kind of something are you hoping for and how will you know it when it arrives? This, if memory serves me correctly, was one of the more enlightening essays you presented to me in your last year as a student here. I was wondering if you had, after thirty years, refined your answer?"

"I believe philosophy is not what I need at the moment. Sorry to disturb you." Stella got to her feet with the intention of leaving.

"Stay. Talk. It has been a while and I am curious," said Socrates

"About?"

"Many things, but one in particular. Why are you still so angry?"

"With all due respect, my business is my own and you are no longer my teacher and I do not need to be lectured to." Even as the words left her mouth Stella knew that she had not meant to say it or to say it in such a sharp tone. She quickly sought to make redress. "Sorry, that is not what I meant to say. I mean I have things on my mind that you do not need to know or worry about. I'll be fine. I am trying to sort things out here before I go back to England and my husband and I had an argument. I just came up here to think."

Socrates said nothing, and although the silence only lasted seconds Stella felt the overwhelming need to fill it with sound. Instead of joining in listening to what the silence could say or reveal, she did what she always did (as most of us do) – she talked.

"I came back to sort out the family estate now that my mother has died and I am the only child. Peter wants us to uproot and move here. Not to sell the house. Not to clear the past away once and for all but to try and engage in some dream whereby we live here. Ridiculous! How would that work? What about my job? I have spent years setting up a practice. I am a psychologist back in England, and do not intend to throw it away on some idealistic, romantic whim. Why should I? It is okay for him, he does not seem to care where he lives or works, he can do that but I can't. How would we cope? What about the friends that I have made in England? Who do I know here any more? If this is such a good place to live why is it only inhabited by old people and those lacking in drive or ambition?"

Socrates said nothing but raised his eyebrows to show that he was either curious or surprised by her comments.

"Oh, I am sorry, I do not mean you. I did not mean to offend. Sometimes I seem to just say the wrong thing at the wrong time. I am sorry, I have to go." Once again Stella made to leave.

"Stay and talk. I would value that. We only have another hour of good light before dusk and this place is most beautiful as the sun sets. Stay. Talk."

Part of Stella was relieved that Socrates had not allowed her bluster and rambling to distract from her need and she sat again on the grass and sad stock.

Silence. Warmth. Stillness and calm.

Stella was reminded that Socrates allowed lots of space and silence during his lessons. Too many in her opinion. While she wanted to get into the cut and thrust of debate Socrates created the space for dialogue, and she was aware that this is what he was doing now.

Silence.

"What do you want?" Socrates repeated.

"I just—"

"Do not be in such a rush to answer. Take a breath. If you are going to say something make sure it is something worth saying. If you spit out your words without time for thought it is like serving food before it is fully cooked or pouring wine before it is ready. Neither food, wine or words will be palatable and will be rejected by the person receiving them."

"I do not want a lesson."

"The person that has stopped learning has stopped living."

The truth of that statement stung her and she could feel her anger rising. She was silent but her fury was deafening.

"Forgive me," Socrates said, after what seemed like an age. "I did not mean to offend you. I find it hard to get out of the habit of teacher, especially with past pupils. Particularly, and please do not think that this is flattery, when I am again in the company of a past pupil who I had real affection and interest for."

This unexpected revelation of love flipped Stella's mood from resentment to confused vulnerability. Why had he said that? She was not aware in her memories and perceptions of her time at school that he held her in affection. She had imagined that he looked down on her because she was forever answering back and failed so often in the tasks he had set her.

The release from the day's heat and her realization that she was in a safe place – not being judged, but being supported, listened to and encouraged – provided the right

57

conditions to touch her sadness, and she began to weep. She spilled the tears that she had kept locked away since hearing of her mother's death. During the past months the tears had been few and short-lived but now they flowed. Unstoppable and hot against her face. Between the retching sobs of relief Stella tried to speak. "Sorry… it's just that… all this time… I do not know if I can… he always… I know he is doing it for the right reasons but he never listens… I can't just up sticks… there is too much to deal with…"

Socrates did not try to stop, calm, reassure or answer her. He allowed time to move forward and for her to get to a point of quiet when the first layer of words had been used and she had reached a place where the silence was unforced, the hearing was clear and the heart was open. After several minutes and as the sky began to change to red as the sun retreated he reminded Stella of why she had come to the tree. Why did she always come to this spot when she needed reassurance and clarity?

"What kind of something are you hoping for and how will you know it when it arrives"

Silence

'I want to be certain that the things that I am doing are the right things. I need to be sure that any action I take is going to be the right action.'

Silence.

Socrates spoke calmly and seriously, as if every word had been weighed out and balanced. "What would happen if you took action based on an uncertainty of the future but driven by your heart and not your logic?"

"Well, I would—"

"Stop." His voice was gentle but firm. "You answered without the space for thought. Take your time and then answer with the right thought. Right thought creates the right words which lead us to the right action."

Stella welcomed the reminder of the dialoguing techniques that had been central to Socrates' lessons. While they had been a frustration to her as a child and young person, now she seemed to crave the discipline of dialoguing. In her job as a psychologist she applied similar techniques to draw thoughts and feelings from her clients. But that was one-sided and this was about creating a balance – an ebb and flow, a real exchange between two people seeking a truth, not wanting to win an argument.

She reflected on the rules (no creativity without a structure, no real dialogue without rules). She thought. She physically relaxed and made sure her response was a statement that finished with open-ended questions to engage Socrates in the dance of dialogue. She did not blurt out whatever was on her mind and close him out with a question that was geared towards a 'yes' or 'no' response. Socrates mirrored this approach and they talked.

Eventually they became aware that the village lights were now cutting through

the dark and it was time to pause in their dialogue. They had not concluded, they had not arrived at any clear goal, but they were both happy with the exchange.

"Come and meet Peter," Stella suggested, as she rose from the sad stock and made to return to the village.

"I would love to, but not now. Prepare food, time and place and then I would love to join you. But not now."

"It is late. Peter and I rarely go to bed before one in the morning."

"This is a good thing, as you two need to continue the dialogue."

"Oh, he will think this all too Greek and dismiss it."

Silence.

Then Stella spoke again. "But that was my past image of him and not the future possibility. I will go and talk and prepare food, time and place for you to join us tomorrow. Join us around midday. That should be enough to start a dialogue."

Socrates smiled, nodded as confirmation, stepped forward and, in the traditional and respectful manner of showing true affection and respect, kissed Stella, as a parent would kiss a child ready for sleep, or as friends that kiss at a time of departure, three times on alternate cheeks.

"Are you not returning to the village?" asked Stella. "It is getting late and cold."

Silence.

"It is," replied Socrates. "I will return to the village later, but need to be by this old tree for a little more time. Go, prepare food, time and place."

Stella smiled and walked briskly towards the home of her past. She could make out the shadow of Peter on the porch and the red dot of a cigarette glowing like a distant lighthouse.

Stella walked towards Peter. He rose and quickly walked down the path to greet her. His pace was quick, stiff and very English. This brusqueness of tone and tempo that sometimes annoyed her at this moment made her smile with real love and appreciation of his uniqueness. She allowed herself to soften and they held each other and kissed with real warmth that signalled apology and a desire to reconnect.

"Thanks for that," Peter said. "Sorry about all the earlier nonsense. Been thinking. You know best when it comes to things around here–"

"No. I think we should talk first. I may still come up with the same conclusion but let us talk first."

"Sounds good."

"Oh, this arrived when you were out." Peter held out a letter addressed to them both from the wife of Stella's former teacher.

"Sad news, I am afraid," continued Peter in a voice lacking in emotion but sincere nevertheless. "Seems like the old boy was hoping that you would pop over and chat while you were here. He did not want to impose but was keen to catch up. Shame. He died three days ago. Great shame. He sounds like someone I would have liked to meet."

Stella's disbelieving voice broke the silence. "Three days ago? But he can't have!" Was her dialogue with his ghost. Did she so need to talk that Socrates delayed his departure?

Silence.

Stella studied the letter to see when the funeral was to take place.

She spoke half in disbelief, half in grief. "Tomorrow, midday. He is going to be buried at the foot of the old olive tree up there on the hill."

Stella pointed to the tree that she had just returned from. It could have been the shadow of the branches silhouetted by the light of the moon but she saw the outline of an old man who appeared to be sitting beneath the tree. His arms were open and his head was tilting forward, nodding with gentle encouragement as if he were talking intently to another or encouraging them to talk.

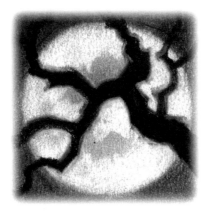

Dialogue: the theory

Roy Leighton

The essence of effective dialogue is the capacity to tell a good story. Better still to tell your story and for it to be heard. Not necessarily to be agreed with, welcomed or applauded but to be heard in order to arrive a little closer to a truth, closer than we were before the story began.

Of course most of us want to talk in order for others to agree or be changed by our words, but that says more about our own ego or inability to change rather than their capacity to listen. Personal evolution is more likely than the transformation of others but still, it seems, we talk to change others rather than ourselves. We, as speakers, seek others to be altered by the power of our oratory. In dialogue the process is about our capacity to listen ourselves as much, if not more, than for others to hear what we have to say.

The interaction between speaker and listener works at many levels. Dialogue – as opposed to 'debate' – is the means by which individuals can move from not knowing to understanding, and from understanding to action. This section will focus on the essential rationale and history of dialogue in order to prepare for some practical exercises to raise the level of dialogue in both our personal and professional environments.

At first glance something so structured as dialogue – particularly Socratic dialogue, so ancient in its history and associated with the perceived stuffy and elite world of academia – is hardly a tool for the speed and rapidity of information exchange that dominates this century.

However, any creative process that seeks to be more than a selfish indulgence designed to show others what one knows or can do needs an order and process in which to evolve. This may seem a contradiction, but when one takes the time to think with structure, process and rules then the foundation is laid for real evolution and elevation of thought. This will usually, although not always, save time, because you do not have to deal with the fall-out, mistakes and arguments that often occur when things have not been clearly explained or understood.

Like all effective teaching dialogue is a balance between order and creative flow. Too much of either can lead to confusion and conflict. When the structure, process and rules become the focus and sight is lost of the purpose, goal or objectives then creativity will be stifled. Indeed, over the hundreds of years since Socrates embarked on his dialogues, too many lofty institutions and academics have subjected the dialoguing process to such painful levels of analysis that its essence has been corrupted. Equally, too much creative flow without the parameters and processes to direct it can become vague, confusing and indulgent.

I do not intend to use this chapter as a way of adding to the mass of pseudo-academic writings that already fill bookshelves and confuse the mind. This chapter is more about moving from awareness to action – from 'knowing' to 'doing'. But part of that process does require an understanding of dialogue structure. So, let us begin.

There are three environments in which we dialogue: by ourselves (inner dialogue); with one other person (intimate dialogue); and with a group (public or collective dialogue). Dialogue in any of these three arenas requires some structure if its outcomes are to be effective.

The other thing to remember about dialogue is that there are three kinds of people with whom we may be having a dialogue: someone who approaches life from a thoughtful, analytical background; someone who seeks to be emotionally and creatively engaged in the process; or someone who needs first of all to find some practical benefit in having a dialogue.

There is an apocryphal story of how Socrates came to realize that there were three core 'types' of people. He was told by the oracle that he was the wisest man in all Athens. So he checked – as, indeed, any truly wise man would. He had dialogues with the thinkers (scholars, politicians, philosophers, and so on), with creatives (artists, musicians, poets, muses, and so on) and with those of a more practical disposition (builders, artisans and athletes). He wanted to get to the 'truth'. Was he truly the wisest man? In order to get to the truth he applied dialogue (through the word) to his conversations. He did not follow the traditional 'debating' approach that would become so popular in the Roman senate, which was more about dominating and seeking to change someone else's point of view without being open to change oneself.

Socrates came to the realization that he was not 'wise' but 'clever'. He knew stuff, and thought a lot, but he was not very creative or artistic, and you would not ask Socrates to put up a shelf. Intelligence – real intelligence – is the ability, given whatever circumstances you find yourself in at any moment, to come up with solutions. It is not just knowing stuff, it is doing something with the stuff you know. This is why Socratic dialogue is still such a powerful tool in the present age, despite its ancient history: we still need to provide a format within which people can communicate, arrive at new understanding and then feel confident to transform that new thinking into action. It was a challenge then and it is a challenge now.

The process of dialoguing has been developed and refined over the years. Plato, the student of Socrates, made the structure clearer during his lifetime and many others have contributed since then. In the last century, one of the most significant of those seeking to define the Socratic method was the eminent German scholar, Leonard Nelson. Nelson is arguably the greatest influence on how dialogue has been applied in modern Western society. Despite linking his technique with Socrates and Plato, Nelson allowed the cultural and historical traits of the time to dominate and adjust the process.

The historical Socrates, as in Plato's early dialogues, never arrives at a robust answer or outcome. Socrates was more into unearthing the truth as one might peel an onion. You may get to a level of understanding but there is always another layer to penetrate. The idea that Socratic method can produce answers actually comes from Plato, who – like any good student – wanted to build on the learning gleaned from his mentor. Plato thought that philosophy was unique among other forms of teaching and learning. He felt that if you could use the structures provided by dialogue then you could arrive at real and powerful insights:

> It [philosophical dialogue] does not at all admit of verbal expression like other studies, but as a result of continued application to the subject itself and communion therewith, it is brought to birth in the soul on a sudden, as light that is kindled by a leaping spark, and thereafter it nourishes itself.
>
> (Plato, *Ep.*, VII:531)

Prior to the Second World War, there was a growing movement in Germany for Socratic thought and true democratic debate. Nelson was one of the leading advocates who sought to bridge the gap between theory and practice. In 1922, he established a

63

boarding school for children (the *Walkemuhle*) and an academy for adult education (the Philosophical-Political Academy – PPA) in order to test his educational concepts in real-life situations. Like Socrates, Plato and others able to lift themselves above mere hypothesis, Nelson believed that dialogue and independent thought *could* change individuals, groups and society.

The staff in Nelson's school and academy used the Socratic method in their professional work. I use a similar approach in my work in education and business, and it is a constant source of amazement to me, and those I work with, much time that you can save so when you invest time, agree on a process, and focus more on the goal than the ego. The section on practical applications that follows this theory will show how to do this.

When you are aware, beyond mere research, of the impact that such a powerful, balanced and engaging process can have upon oneself, on others and the environment, it can lead to a revolution in your own thinking and action. It can also be seen as a threat to those who seek control through dogmatic thought and inflexible structures, as Nelson's followers found to their own cost when in 1933, six years after his death, the organization founded by Nelson was banned by the Nazi regime and forced underground.

Many who had attended Nelson's academy and joined the political movement he founded became active underground anti-fascists in opposition to Hitler. Susanne Miller, a German historian, has written about the importance of participation in Socratic dialogues during those dark, repressive and regressive times. It was this participation that sustained those who took part in the underground resistance, enabling them to retain and deepen their inner convictions in the fight for survival under Nazi tyranny. In 1949 the PPA, but not the school for children, was re-established in Germany.

While I would not compare our current society to the repressive regime of pre-war Nazi Germany (although there are some that would), our new global family has brought with it new challenges and a great need for listening, questioning and reason. In an age of shallow, egocentric reasoning and short-term gratification it has never been more important to have a structured means of approaching our global complexity through the capacity to dialogue and not just debate.

Rene Saran and Barbara Neisser (2004) speak of the value that Socratic dialogue has for encouraging ordinary human reflection. Such dialogue can be an extremely powerful experience for people of all backgrounds. What makes it special is that it is open to people of any age or background who wish to engage in a co-operative thinking activity where the basic aims are:

● To answer a philosophical question by seeking out the truth about the nature of concepts like tolerance, freedom, justice and responsibility, and to endeavour to reach consensus – that is, to reach a result or outcome.

● To engage in the co-operative activity of seeking answers to questions and to understand each other through the explora-tion of concrete experiences, volunteered by participants, one of which is usually chosen by the group for detailed analysis. In this way all are engaged in the process.

● To deepen individual insights and understandings as the dialogic process moves towards enabling participants to grasp the moral perplexities of the everyday world.

● To gain through dialogue greater clarity about what is and what is not in keeping with considered, thoughtful and reason-able conduct, thus enhancing self-confidence in our ability to reason and so shaping our approach to life.

Although Socratic dialogue may not lead to a definite outcome in the form of agreed answers, this need not lead to disappointment. It is the positive experience of participation in co-operative thinking that is of such major importance. Saran and Neisser emphasize its value as a learning process which can have profound meaning for one's life, since genuine conversation demands a real willingness to work towards truth with others who are pursuing the same aim. It is this openness to truly listen with a desire to see the world as it is and not just as we imagine it is that lies at the heart of sincere, mature adult interaction.

Jonathan Sacks, in his enlightening work *The Dignity of Difference* (2002), reinforces the importance of engaging in dialogue without being driven to reach a point of finality and agreement. The process of dialogue is more than getting to a shared point of agreement, it is about having a shared experience and being open to have your view of the world challenged:

> We must make ourselves open to their [people from different traditions and beliefs] stories, which may profoundly conflict with ours. We must even, at times, be ready to hear of their pain, humiliation and resentment and discover that their image of us is anything but our image of ourselves. We must learn the art of conversation, from which truth emerges not, as in Socratic dialogues, by the refutation of falsehood but from the quite different process of letting our world be enlarged by the presence of others who think, act and interpret reality in ways radically different from our own.

The next section shows how to begin to achieve this.

65

Dialogue: the exercises

Roy Leighton

The aim of this final section on dialogue is action-based. Its purpose is to take the theory and put it into practice. Most of us think of 'dialogue' as taking place between two people, but it always starts with one: ourself. It is hugely important to enter into dialogue with others having given some time to listening to ourself. Why are we having this dialogue and what is its purpose? Do we want learning and insight or just a good argument?

Know why you are having the dialogue in the first place. I like the image of a 'star' and a 'mountain' to highlight the focus for purposeful dialogue. Imagine the star is your big vision, mission or purpose. This is your driving force in your life. The reason you do the things you do. Why you do the job you do. Why you are with the people and communities you are with. The star is always there and illuminates our actions at both a conscious and subconscious level.

Think of the mountain as the task or challenge you now face. It can be a daily, weekly or a monthly mountain but it is the thing that you have to get over. When dialogue is clear and focused on a specific outcome motivated by a greater purpose, then the time spent in dialogue is much more rich, enlightening and effective.

The question here is 'Does your mountain support your star?'. In other words, are you doing things in your life that are in alignment with your goal, mission, vision or whatever you may call it? If not, why are you spending time on a mountain that does not move you closer to your star? That is a good open-ended question to kick off a bit of philosophical enquiry.

What do we do when we have climbed the mountain? Well, some people are so relieved they climb the same one again and again and again. Others sit on top of the mountain that they have climbed proclaiming that some day, when the time is right, they will climb another one. One of those. Over there. Probably that big one. Some day.

Adults (an adult being someone who is comfortable to evolve by challenging their own thinking, behaviour and world view), having reached the top of their mountain stop, admire where they have come from and what lies ahead. They then take a breath and start a new ascent.

Dialoguing is the process for assisting us and others in choosing the right mountains.

Inner dialogue – the B-movie syndrome

Confidence, or lack of it, depends on three factors: ourselves, others and the environment. When we are in the right place, at the right time, doing the right thing with the right people, we feel there is nothing that we cannot achieve. However, when we are with people that do not seem to see the world as we do, when we are engaged in a task that we are not committed to or comfortable with, or when we feel that our time (life) is being wasted, then it is time to rethink.

We all have two voices in our heads (some of us may have a few more!), and one of the voices is saying 'You are great, beautiful, talented and here for a purpose'. The other is saying 'Today is the day they find out how stupid you are'. I have that voice at the moment. As I write this I am struggling with a dialogue in my head between me and a former teacher. He stopped me when I was fifteen, and just about to sit my English O-level, and said, "Don't worry about your spelling and your handwriting, Leighton. People from your council estate don't go to university.' I failed the exam. I have written a couple of successful books and published many articles, and I regularly have to submit programme outlines, plans and reports, yet even now I still have to work on silencing the voice that says that I should not be doing this. It is getting easier, but the voice is still there.

This fear is something I think of as the B-movie syndrome, and it is a major factor in preventing us from understanding and expressing ourselves. The negative aspect of our imagination can conjure up events that are upsetting and harmful. Our fear of what might happen often prevents us from taking action. 'Fear' gives us a useful acronym to summarize this state: False Expectations Appearing Real. Our amazingly creative mind can cause us to imagine such a false outcome to our potential actions that we do not act.

The exercise I describe here enables us to check what our inner voice is telling us and judge whether it is worth listening to. It taps into what Howard Gardner, in his work on multiple intelligences, terms *intrapersonal* intelligence: the capacity to stop, reflect, rethink

67

and then take new action. While most of us can see this is an important first step, few of us create time for it because we mistake immediate action for genuine progress. The whole basis of a good dialogue is to create the space, time and stillness to enable clarity of thought.

I have devised this exercise for you, dear reader, but it can be done with students at Key Stage 3 and above, and adapted for Key Stages 1 and 2. Many children get over-anxious when taking tests and if they can get into the habit of breathing deeply, slowing their heart rate and bringing oxygen to the brain, then their capacity for recall is significantly improved. The exercise is broken into three stages and should be conducted in a time and place where you know you are not going to be disturbed.

Once you have studied the stages of this exercise (I have set it out as if you were delivering it to a group), do it for yourself so that you can understand the benefit practically.

- Working with a group of about 20 or less, make sure everyone has a chair and that they are sitting in a circle. Ask them to turn their chairs around so they are facing outwards.

- Explain that you are going to introduce them to an exercise that is over 2,000 years old and originates from ancient Egypt. It will enable them, if they practise it regularly (ideally daily), to compose their minds. This will help them in many situations but it is a particularly good exercise for reducing panic in exams and interview situations and for producing a clear head for discussion and dialogue.

- Ask them to sit up straight (making sure that their backs are supported by the chair). Ask them to imagine that they have an invisible thread holding them up from the crown of their heads, keeping it steady and free of tension. Ask them to rest their hands on their thighs and place their feet flat on the floor. It is important that they are not so much 'relaxed' but free of tension and firmly balanced.

- Ask them to breathe in to the count of five seconds, hold it for three more, and then exhale for six seconds. Their breath should come through their nose, and they should imagine it going down their spine to their stomachs, where it is held for the count of three and then exhaled, coming up the front of their bodies and out of their mouths. Talk them through their breathing, counting their breath in and out. If anyone is showing obvious signs of physical tension, for example, raised shoulders, a stiff neck, head tilted back or chin pointing upwards, encourage them to stretch and release their muscles and to try to visualize the thread giving them support.

- When they have got into a regular breathing rhythm, ask them to drop their right hand so their arm is hanging limply by their side. Keep reminding them to focus on their breathing.

- Explain that you want them to imagine the flow of blood from their heart. The blood is being pumped from the heart up to the right-hand side of their body. It is travelling down the arm till it reaches the fingertips, where it changes direction, travels back up the arm and continues on its journey around the body. Ask them to focus on their fingertips.

- They will begin to feel a tingling sensation in the tips of their fingers; they are to focus on this. If the muscles in their arm are relaxed the tingling will get stronger. Encourage them to release the arm even more, to breath deeply and regularly and develop a stronger tingling sensation.

When they reach this state they are physically ready to engage their imagination, logic and memory. That is to say they are ready to create new possibilities, solve problems, recall facts and have a dialogue, being clear about the mountain they are climbing and the star that is motivating them.

One-to-one dialogue – intimate relationships

While debate is more about speaking to inform and persuade, dialogue is about listening and being changed. Dialogue is very much a balance between ourselves and others. The main focus is the listening and attention we give to the other person as they speak. Effective dialogue is where you focus on hearing and thinking and this needs space and order. To do this well you both need to play by the same rules.

On the next page is a structure for dialogue that draws on the ideas of Socrates (469–399 BC). When working with students, sell them this profound and serious technique as if it is a game. Rehearse the structure by keeping the questions asked simple and fun. Each person has to build on what the other person has said and should not go

off on some unrelated journey. How many of us are not interested in what the other person has to say but just waiting for them to finish so that we can talk about ourselves? The basic structure for beginning and sustaining dialogue looks like this:

Person A: Gives some information, opinion or comment.
A then asks an open question of person B that is related to the information A has just presented.

Person B: Waits and thinks for a minimum of 5 seconds then answers.
B then gives more information, opinion or comment and asks an open question of A that builds on the information and subject presented. B is not to bring in completely unrelated facts, events or ideas but has to hold the focus of the dialogue.

Person A: Waits and thinks for a minimum of 5 seconds then answers.
A then gives more information, opinion or comment and asks an open question of B.

Get the students to practise this structure for a few minutes.

Next, check whether the questions asked were open or closed. Open questions encourage a more undirected response, and those people who use lots of 'closed' questions are, consciously or not, focusing more on manipulating the conversation to their own ends. If people can answer 'yes' or 'no' to a question then the question is 'closed'. For example, 'did you', 'do they', 'is this', and so on. Open questions would begin with 'who', 'what', 'where', 'when', 'why' or 'how'. Notice how often in daily conversations you tend to steer people into a yes or no response.

Continue the dialogue, this time making sure that the 5-second rule is applied and that open-ended questions are used. If someone asks a closed question or does not wait the 5 seconds then the dialogue buddy needs to indicate this to them. When working with students I introduce an imaginary buzzer. If someone does not wait or asks a closed question then the other person makes a buzzer-like noise. While this is fun it also signals to the brain that not listening and not questioning openly will get a negative response – a bit of neural reprogramming at work here.

After a few minutes of dialoguing and buzzing, get feedback from the group on how this feels. Some will very much like working in this way, but for others it is totally alien. Remind them that this is not simply a chat but a systematic process for arriving at a greater understanding and truth. If you do not want to understand and are more concerned with keeping your view of the world unaltered do not learn this skill. It is, in a very real sense, potentially mind- if not life-changing.

And so it continues until a consensus has been agreed. If running this exercise with a group, give them some time to become comfortable with the process before focusing on a specific idea, problem or philosophical question.

If you really want to have a good dialogue you must set aside time to achieve this: this time can vary based on the seriousness of the topic. You can have short bursts of dialogue over a coffee or meal. Avoid pairing dialogue with drink as the two seldom work. Of course, Socrates might disagree with this, being one for the wine!

How long for an effective dialogue? Well, it can vary. Most dialogue is focused on the collective mountain and therefore the dialogues can be of a realistic duration (from a few minutes to a few hours). When you start talking about 'stars' then you are probably looking at several dialogues over weeks, months and years. Socrates said that a good dialogue should take about two days. That is why, if you want to reconnect to the big vision and plan a strategy for dealing with your immediate mountains, you should try to set aside a whole weekend. Ask yourself when you and your partner or team last took a couple of days out just to talk and listen? Maybe one of the outcomes of this chapter might be to book a weekend mini-break.

Let us now look at the stages in preparing for good dialogue and making the most of the time you have.

Group talk – having a forum

Good dialogue takes place in a forum and involves a group of people, facilitated by a person who manages the process and the group. This could be a teacher or, depending on the experience and maturity of the class, it could be a student. This exercise works across the Key Stages.

First establish the purpose (mountain) for the dialogue: for example, 'We are here to discuss the impact of study time for teachers in the timetable' or 'Why is being open-minded important to learning?'.

When people are clear on the goal, sit people in a complete or semi-circle (just think Greek theatre), where everyone can see and hear everyone else. You may want to get the students to do the relaxation exercise highlighted above as preparation.

Go round the circle and ask people to say how they feel about the question or task. We all respond to new events and information emotionally first, and this needs to be recognized. Do not interrupt or allow anyone else to interrupt, tut, sneer, make negative remarks or in any way make a value judgement on the speaker's contribution.

It is vital that the rules of respect and value are established and upheld throughout. If they are not then the door to dialogue runs the risk of becoming very firmly shut. Children – just like all of us, in fact – are loath to open their mouths to speak if the reaction they get is dismissive, destructive or degrading.

Find an object which is to be held by the person speaking. This is a simple but very effective tool for focusing the attention of the group on the speaker. Just think of the importance of the shell for the boys in William Golding's novel *Lord of the Flies*. If you have the conch, you can talk.

If people want to talk they indicate this to the forum leader (that's you), who will decide who speaks and when. Do not always give the 'conch' according to who put their hands up first. If you set a 'hands up first – speak first' precedent you will fall into a trap in which those who feel comfortable putting their hands up at every opportunity will talk too much. Instead, you can create opportunities by passing the object to the more shy or intrapersonally oriented child or adult, thus drawing them into the dialogue.

These group forums are always enlightening whatever Key Stage you work with.

It is important to leave time to close the session in a structured way, so that people are all clear about what was discussed and what action is to be taken. At the end of each of the sessions:

- Summarize what has been discussed

- Point to the action that is going to be taken as a result of the dialogue. If no action is going to be taken then you have to ask yourself what the point of the dialogue was. The action could just be that people will go away and think more about what they said and heard, and return to the next session with feedback. This then provides a starting point for the next session, and links the dialogues together if this is what is wanted.

- Thank people for their contribution. This might seem so obvious that it does not need stating but often we cause a block to moving forward because we do not give value and thanks to where we are and how we got here.

Deepening the dialogue

The above sections deal with the basic structures for effective dialogues for ourselves and others. Below is a summary of additional facets that you should seek to build in to refine and improve effective dialoguing skills.

Time

Always create time for dialogue rather than cramming it in while multitasking. If you are doing other things rather than giving time to the task this devalues the person with whom you are seeking to dialogue. Too many squeezed-in seconds will result in people not feeling as if they are able to talk to you.

When working with groups with a deadline give everyone equal time to talk, indicating to them when they have a minute to finish. Three-minute chunks to get people's key thoughts and feelings should be sufficient and you can always go round the group several times focusing on what they think, how they feel and what action do they think should be taken.

Attention

Listen as if what they are saying is interesting and relevant. If it is not then the effort you make to show them that what they are saying is interesting and relevant will likely (but not guaranteed) enable people to open up and talk at an interesting and relevant level.

Feed back to them the essence of what they have been saying before coming to any action points or conclusions. So, you might begin your summing up something like this: 'So, let me just be clear about what you are saying…'. Check that this is what they are saying and allow them space to edit, amend or clarify and then repeat 'So, let me just be clear…'. When you are clear and they are reassured then whatever action points or suggestions you make will be heard and more likely to be completed without wasting time having to go back and make the points again, often, by making time to talk, we avoid future misunderstandings and time-wasting.

Place

Find a place to talk that gives value to the dialogue. The physical environment greatly impacts people's capacity to open up. When I work with schools I often take people out to talk somewhere nice and share food. Bombarding someone with nice sights, sounds, tastes, textures and smells has often proven to provide the environment where people feel valued and at ease. When someone is open and valued then dialogue can occur. Where people are distracted by a negative multisensory environment then dialogue is much more of an effort and much less effective.

Finally

Good dialogue, like all skills, takes effort, and I would encourage you to practise a little and often, in order to refine these skills until they become second nature. As Socrates would say:

> The shortest and surest way to live with honour in the world is to be in reality what we would appear to be; and if we observe, we shall find, that all human virtues increase and strengthen themselves by the practice of them.

74

The child and the dragon

Steve Bowkett

The boy who would one day be an enchanter took the wooden shield and sword that his father had made for him and went out to play. He walked right to the bottom of the garden at the back of the house. It was a walled garden and from the earliest years of his life it had contained all that he'd ever known. More recently his elders had encouraged him to go beyond those walls.

"But I feel comfortable on this side of them," the child had protested. His mother had nodded and smiled – it was a gesture that could mean anything, the boy knew full well.

"Yes, and that's why you must go beyond them. All in good time, of course."

Now, thinking back, he smiled and wondered if there was such a thing as "all in bad time"? But he wasn't in the mood to ponder this. Instead, he drew his sword, lifted his shield and attacked the fierce dragon that lay curled around the roots of the nearby rowan tree.

The dragon was guarding a treasure hoard, which was their function, so he'd been told. The boy swished his blade around the beast's iridescent green head and made stabbing movements towards its dozing, half-closed eyes. For a time nothing at all happened and the boy grew frustrated. But then the lid of the dragon's left eye lifted a little, just enough to show the golden gleam of the eye itself. Oh, polished brighter than the brightest brass, giving out its own light, it seemed, its centre dark as a night without stars – and in the far, far depths a red spark that might have been a flicker of the devil's own fire.

The boy leaped back with a cry. It had only been a pretend dragon after all, a make-believe monster that was surely no more real than the dark-robed figure suddenly standing nearby.

The boy gasped and his whole body felt cold just for an instant, then hot with the flush of imagined misdemeanours.

"Sir, forgive me. I was only—" He hesitated, feeling foolish to say it. "I was only playing. It was only make-believe."

"Making beliefs," said the tall, dark-robed stranger. "Isn't that what children are supposed to do?"

The boy was hardly listening. He had noticed that the stranger's shadow seemed to blend with his own. And both were cast towards the rowan tree, as though pointing at it. And, daring to look a little more boldly, he decided that this tall man with his gaze wise as a quiet spring day was familiar. Something about him reminded the child of his own self; something far removed but never apart.

"Words make actions. Actions make lives," said the man. "Did you know," he went on with a sudden enthusiasm, "that the word 'dragon' means 'bright' and 'to see'? And it may be connected to the very old word *darsayati*, 'he causes to see'?"

The boy shrugged and shook his head. "I never knew that."

"Well now you will never not know it." And the man smiled a child-at-play smile and seemed very pleased with himself.

And so it was that the white-haired stranger and the yellow-haired boy quickly became friends. They sat against the rowan trunk, taking good care not to disturb the slumbering dragon just yet. And the man told the child stories of places far and wide, near and narrow, and of adventures that were filled with daring and excitement and the tumbling of gods' dice; and of choices deliberately made; and of joy and pain and of regrets that were never allowed to be born.

"You have lived a marvellous life," said the boy at last. They'd sat for a long time, but something about the day had changed. The lovely spring sun was past its high point and the quality of the light was different now. Late afternoon had become earliest evening. The boy smelt honeysuckle and the air felt the tiniest degree cooler.

"And so will you," proclaimed the stranger, as though he knew for sure. "Because you are a wonder, child. A wonderchild. It is all before you, but for the getting there. Talking of which—" And here the man pushed himself painfully to his feet and his old joints crackled with stiffness. "I think we need to find out what this dragon is hiding, eh?"

That brought a new fear flashing through the boy's heart. What had seemed only a game had now turned into something serious and maybe dangerous. Something with consequences. He began to think of problems immediately. They crowded into his thoughts and made him tremble.

"But what if—?"

The old man laughed delightedly. "Two of those words are the most important of all. The third you can throw away. To imagine before we create. How else could it be?"

There was such a sense of joy in the man's tone that the boy could not help himself but agree. The man – not the stranger, for he was no longer one of those – took up a rowan twig and waved it around and about. The dragon swirled away into shadow; the rowan roots seemed to ease aside, and there was a cleft in the sun-warmed earth and man and child were diving down into the space between here and there and now and then.

Blink – and the boy was in a cellar and his companion was nowhere to be seen. But instead there was a wizard – a wysard, a wise old man – who might have been the boy's newfound friend or even the boy himself, one day.

The wizard seemed to be busy mixing up potions and trying out all sorts of different magics. Delicate lightnings streaked from his fingers. Some of them flickered along the walls and ceiling, which was a mass of tangled roots leading up – the child presumed – to the very rowan tree where the adventure had begun.

Some of the lightning sparks came to a stop and lay twinkling on the stones or hung in spiders' webs like nets of fine jewels. The boy realized that many forces were involved in the wizard's work. He wasn't simply making sparks and lights. But seemed to be drawing energy up from an even greater depth.

"Can I ask—?" the boy began to say. The wizard flicked out a finger and a dazzle of light splashed blindingly into the child's face, and suddenly he was reunited with his companion, sinking through layers to the underbasement rooms below where the wizard had been working. In this dark and mysterious cellar space, lit faintly by the glow of old enchantment, countless books and stories were stored. The boy ran his gaze along the shelves and saw that they stretched away and away and vanished into far distances beyond the confines of what should have been an individual vault.

"These ideas are shared by the dreaming minds of all people everywhere." The man's voice broke the gentle silence. "From these ancient scripts new stories are made, which help us to remember where we have come from and where we are going. But, you see, the new books contain the wisdom of these older stories too. And the new tellings are added to this storehouse so that the wisdom grows and can be explained many times over in many different ways. Such is the work of the mages and sages who maintain the fabric of this place."

"You mean," the boy said, "there are lots of them?"

"Uncountable numbers of them."

The child was intrigued. "And they write these books?" The old man nodded. "But who wrote the first book?"

"Now you are asking important questions," the man said. "And there isn't one answer upon which all are agreed. Some say that the original book happened by accident, through the tumbling of particles in the ancient oceans. Others think that in the beginning there was spoken the very first word and this gave rise to all the other words you'll find in every one of these volumes. Nobody knows for sure – or even if they do, they can't prove it to other wizards who might disagree." The old man shrugged. "Such is life. But enough of these dark and hidden places. Time I think to climb out of here."

The boy looked up at the mass of intricate roots. "It looks like a very hard climb," he said.

"That's why it's worth doing," his friend and mentor replied.

So they climbed into the evening sunlight, up and up until the world was a flat map of white trackways and little green patches and grey wrinkled hills. The horizons curved away round into a smoky haze, a sight that was dizzying even though the comforting cover of leaves and branches helped to take away the breathtaking sense of infinite space.

"Wow!" said the boy, and clung close to his friend's dark robes, which fluttered about in the cool, just-night wind. It had been a long and hard journey, but with every move he gained greater height and a better perspective. The boy reached out to grab a branch, then found a better handhold and took that instead.

"Do you see how it's up to each of us to make our way?" The old man's voice swept by on a gusting breeze. "We come to many points where the branches split, and here a decision needs to be made. That's how it is. We choose, and we are defined by our choices. But always we go onward – and upward too, if we remember where we have come from and think about where we want to go."

78

The old man climbed a little higher up and a little farther in. The boy followed his friend's progress. But then his gaze moved beyond that to take in the infinity of branches spreading out into the darkening sky. And along the branches right to their very tips the stars sparkled like seeds hung across the glowing canopy of heaven.

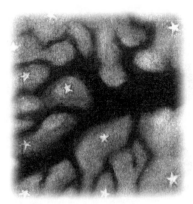

Soon afterwards the child opened his eyes and yawned. His back was sore where he had been resting against the knobbly trunk of the tree. His wooden shield and sword lay beside him, unused. He wondered if his imagination had run away with him. Maybe it would be better, he thought, if he ran away with his imagination.

He scrambled up stiffly, gathered his playthings, and stood for some moments thinking about the wizard, his friend. The old man had shown him that the dragon had been of the boy's own making, a thing of confusions and doubts. It guarded nothing that could not be reached by the statement drawn upon the shield and the question etched on the sword's bright blade and the will to use them, which was something that lay in the child's own heart. There was no barrier. The way was open to everyone.

The boy looked around. The walled garden seemed very small now, yet cosy – still and safe and familiar. He could always return here if the big wide world proved to be rather too daunting.

But for now the day's adventures were done and tea would no doubt be ready. Sheathing his sword, shouldering his shield, the child turned around and walked back towards his home.

Narrative intelligence

Steve
Bowkett

Theories

The creative attitude is not just about being nosy in order to generate ideas, but also creating contexts within which ideas have greater meaning and power to solve problems. This section focuses on that aspect of our thinking.

Multiple intelligences

Many people involved with education are familiar with Howard Gardner's 'multiple intelligences' model of how the mind works (Gardner, 1993). As I read it, essentially Gardner says that 'intelligence' has been too narrowly defined in schools, emphasizing as it does the more conscious critical thinking skills, coupled with students' ability to retain and reiterate facts on demand under formalized conditions.

Gardner asserts that such an 'IQ'-type definition vastly underestimates the human mind's power and potential. He proposes that instead we define intelligence as our ability to handle information. 'Handle' to me means the active *manipulation* of ideas (*manus* is Latin for 'hand') – 'getting one's hands on' the stuff of thinking. This dynamic involvement with ideas *is* the in-forming process of evolving more robust and flexible meanings and more sophisticated understandings of the world mentioned in my earlier chapter.

Gardner further suggests that we handle information across a naturally occurring range of domains of knowledge and understanding. 'Naturally occurring' implies that we are all born with our brains 'hard-wired' to understand the world in these ways. If I am curious about words; if I notice how language can create images in my mind -- evoking feelings and triggering memories, bringing about new mental links, changing my perspectives; if I'm prepared to explore and play with language to see what I can create with it; and if I notice the effects of my words on other people, then that approach to language is the best way to develop what Gardner calls my 'linguistic intelligence'. In other words, my *ability* to handle information conveyed through words develops *as* I handle information conveyed through words. This, I think, is the essence of 'learning by doing', and it is fully congruent with the creative/thinking approach to education that I've been trying to outline.[1]

Gardner's model is a powerful organizing idea that helps to inform the strategies behind practical and effective learning-to-learn programmes. Other equally valuable insights stem from the work of Kieran Egan (1997, 2002), who has long recognized the links between creative thinking, the power and diversity of the imagination and the use of subconscious resources. However, while Gardner's theories emphasize the areas in which understanding occurs, Egan's work focuses on how understanding develops through childhood and on into adulthood.

Egan's hierarchy of understandings

It is a truism that we are born into the world with virtually no knowledge or experience of it but with a huge potential to make meanings or, to paraphrase John Abbott's comment, to create 'informed theories of everything' (Abbott and Ryan, 2000). As Marshall McLuhan said many years ago, humans are 'meaning-making creatures'. Our ability to do this well is the secret of our success both individually and as a species. Egan asserts that our intelligence allows us to handle many kinds of information, and that we handle it in different ways as we grow. His 'hierarchy of understandings' thesis looks like this.

1   Our earliest understanding is *somatic* understanding, where we understand directly through our bodies. Babies 'know' that they are hot or cold, hungry or thirsty, upset or comforted. The meanings we make are referenced through the flesh.

2   As mental abilities develop and experience grows we evolve a *mythic* understanding. For young children the world is full of mystery and wonder. In order to make sense they mythologize, they make up stories to explain things. This process corresponds to the notion of 'naïve theories'. Storymaking is thus already a powerful means of contextualizing, of creating understanding in the absence of extensive experience and knowledge.

3   Older children, armed with emergent conscious critical faculties, display *romantic*
    understanding of the world. Here children perhaps recognize the naivety of their
    myths: certainly the stories must be refined as knowledge and conscious ability
    increase. Romantic understanding is still driven by a sense of wonder (an essential
    motivation for all enquiry) but this is moderated by the need to find limits and
    boundaries; to create paradigms that act as frameworks for further experience.

4   *Philosophic* understanding typifies adult perspectives, resting on knowledge and
    wisdom usually expressed through language, articulating the map of reality in a
    linear-sequential way. In more sophisticated individuals such linguistic frameworks
    are often rich and robust. They sustain understanding, but unless we question,
    doubt and reflect on them they can be cages rather than supporting structures. If
    the metaphors that underpin our perceptual filters (that help us make sense of
    things) are not challenged we may suffer from what's been called a 'hardening of
    the categories'. By failing to question our mindsets we leave our minds set. For
    example, our understanding of the universe has moved away from the Newtonian
    model, based on the metaphor of the-universe-as-machine, to a quantum-theory
    model that understands it through the metaphor of energy fields. We should (in
    any case) not trap ourselves into thinking we are in possession of ultimate truths or
    be too confident of the (ultimate) reality of what we perceive.

5   According to Egan *ironic* understanding is the pinnacle of our human ability to
    make sense of things. Such understanding is flexible, playful, exploratory,
    challenging, and sometimes mischievous – in the same way as the mythical Trickster
    archetype brings a subversive energy to human attempts to explain the world.
    Ironic understanding embodies two key elements of creativity: the ability to in-form
    oneself, to make mental links that have not been made before; and the ability to
    look at concepts, problems, and so on, from a range of perspectives.

In the same way that forgotten experiences are not lost but are simply influencing on
another (subconscious) level, so I think we never lose our capacity to understand in any of
the ways mentioned above. We are layered and complex creatures.

Contexts of understanding

Stories have been the seedbeds of and training grounds for human understanding (to mix
metaphors) for thousands of years. They communicate on many levels – they resonate
with the multiple ways human understanding occurs. They have a logical-sequential
structure that we understand and appreciate consciously, but they are also 'holistic'
insofar as each offers a complete context within which insights and understandings are
made and conveyed. Stories also stir the emotions, introducing a feeling component that
contributes to their overall meaning for us. And while we may forget the details of stories
(though not necessarily – the most powerful stories linger in the memory for years), the
whole experience can lead to sudden realizations and serve to change our perceptions

forever.[2] In short, stories provide valuable 'packages of meaning' that are quickly and often profoundly assimilated into the subconscious map of reality, thus forming our individual fundamental narrative, our 'life story' if you will.

However, the point of this section is not to argue for the educational value of fictional tales, or to launch a polemic against the fragmentary and hyper-analytical way in which story is approached in many schools. Rather, I want to extend the idea (developed by Egan and others) that *narrative structures* offer the ideal context for developing children's intelligences as they grow through the hierarchy of understandings outlined above, providing frameworks of reference for the application of students' creativity across the age, ability and subject range in schools.

Neurological levels

Another model for human experience is the neurological levels idea devised by Robert Dilts, a pioneer in the field of NLP. This elegant framework identifies six levels at which a person can be functioning. Each level is more abstract than the one below it but has a greater influence on the individual. In ascending order the neurological levels are

1 *environment* – where and when things happen

2 *behaviour* – what we actually do, our actions/responses

3 *capability* – how we do things (our 'cope-ability'), our strategies and techniques in action

4 *belief* – why we do the things we do, including our motivations for action

5 *identity* – who we think we are on a more personal level, our individual sense of self (our 'I-dentity')

6 *spirituality* – who we think we are (and 'why we think we are') in relation to all else that exists.

We might think of a human being as a set of nested Russian dolls, with spirituality lying at the core of each of us and environment operating on a surface level. But as the model implies, each of us is embedded in the universe at large: what we do has consequences on a larger scale, and what happens on the larger scale returns to influence each of us. That kind of layering might be imagined thus:

● immediate environment in time and space (here-and-now)

● 'neighbourhood' environment (community)

● family, including ancestors (blood – or immediate genetic – community)

● the Earth and humanity (the community of the species)

● universe (the community of all life and meaning in the field of space and time).

83

The combination of these ideas can be visualized, as in Fig. 2.1. Now imagine curling the paper round so that the neurological (internal) level of 'spirituality' touches the external level of 'universe'. This little trick emphasizes that the two things (states? – processes?) are not distant from one another, but are actually very closely connected, indeed inseparable. This idea lies at the core of the world's great spiritual traditions and teachings.[3]

Fig 2.1   Neurological levels and our embeddedness in the universe

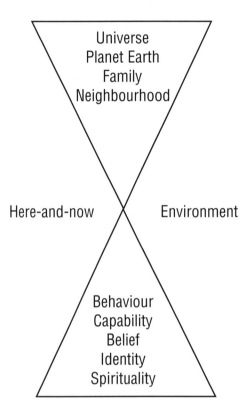

The neurological levels model and the field of NLP itself are relatively recent developments in thinking. But they have their roots in ancient wisdom. Zen philosophy, for instance, views the individual in terms of appearance–heart–intentions (see Brazier, 2001). Put those in the neurological levels triangle with appearance at the top and the similarity of the insights is startling.

By the same token, there is an ancient thread running through the oral tradition of storytelling called 'the ladder to the moon'.[4] This links mundane stories with tales that explore on an increasingly broader canvas, taking in neighbourhood, community, ancestry, mystery and the unexplained, legend and the fantastical and ending with sacred stories and creation myths. The hierarchical nature of this is obvious. So too is the powerful metaphor of the narrative 'ladder' which, through story, leads us in simple steps from the here-and-now to the deepest questions of purpose and existence. Fig. 2.2 illustrates the ladder in more detail.

The ladder to the moon   **Fig 2.2**

Here-and-now

Implications and applications

The triangle as a visual organizer

Visual organizers form a powerful strategy for 'whole brain understanding'. Look again at Fig. 2.1. The bottom-up triangle displays the neurological levels sequentially and hierarchically so that the information can be understood logically at once. But the triangle also draws the eye to its peak or point of focus – the here-and-now – and then broadens awareness as it opens out to illustrate the expanding nature of the external world. Both triangles, forming the hourglass shape, create a strong visual symbol that emphasizes the points being made in the text. Further applications of the triangle organizer are described below.

Themes to motifs

Fig. 2.3 offers a template for planning and/or analysing narratives from either a bottom-up or top-down perspective, starting from the bottom up in this case

> **Themes** indicate the basic level on which narrative is built. They form the foundations of the whole organization of ideas.
>
> **Elements**. This term refers to the basic structural elements of narrative – the load-bearing girders sunk into thematic foundations. Important work in this area was carried out by the folklorist Vladimir Propp (2001). He was intrigued to notice

Fig 2.3   Triangle organizer: themes to motifs

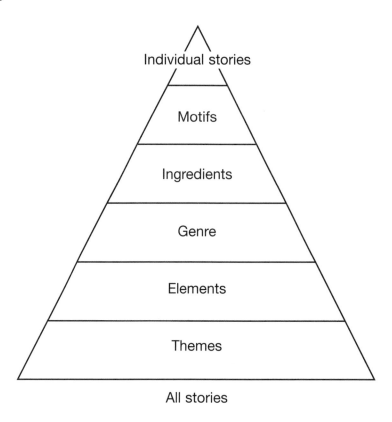

broad similarities between folk tales separated sometimes by continents and millennia – the same kinds of narratives arose in widely divergent societies. Propp's comparative study of thousands of stories from around the world revealed that the most powerful and enduring stories are built around the following framework of elements:

● Hero. The protagonist, representing the force of good, and noble qualities.

● Villain. The antagonist, the hero's negative opposite.

● Problem. A complication created by the villain (or sometimes by circumstances, but exploited by the villain for evil purposes), which the hero must resolve. 'Resolve' in the sense of 're-solve', indicating the cyclical nature of the human condition. Problems arise and are 'solved anew' by each generation.

● Journey. In stories this is usually a physical journey through time and space. For the reader it is always a journey of the imagination. In narrative more broadly speaking, it is a symbolic journey where the hero's qualities and the strategies for resolution are tested, often to the extreme.

● Partner(s). These are subsidiary but significant characters. They can offer alternative viewpoints and strategies, act as sounding boards for the main characters, and can motivate further action and direction. In story they serve to introduce dialogue and subplot in a natural and organic way.

- Help. This element contributes in many ways. Help may come in the form of other characters who themselves offer fresh perspectives and information. Or it can appear as happenstance and accident. In the world of myth and legend and in fantasy fiction the gods look down on the mortal world and so the help can be of a supernatural/spiritual kind.

- Knowledge and power. This often takes the form of the gaining and losing of advantage.

- Object. This may be a physical object that must be found and brought home, or returned elsewhere, or sometimes destroyed. Fragments of the object might need to be separately gathered (each subsidiary journey supplying obstacles and learnings). In all cases narratively speaking, 'object' refers symbolically to the intention of the hero's quest, which is to reach the fixed goal that is the resolution of the problem.

In terms of developing students' story-writing skills, if they bear Propp's elements in mind they will always have a robust framework on which to base their tales.

Genre. This is the narrative level of 'domain', in one sense meaning 'kind of' story – so that we have the genre of Science Fiction, Fantasy, Horror, and so on. More broadly genre refers to the educational domain of a subject area and, more broadly still, to an 'intelligence' or domain of understanding.

Ingredients. This is the level of 'emotional flavouring' within a genre or area of enquiry. In story, the emotional tone is composed of ingredients. These include humour, menace, mystery, excitement, danger, and so on.

Motifs. 'Motif' is also etymologically linked with 'motive', but for our purposes here means 'a constituent feature'. Motifs are the small-scale details that combine to define, describe and distinguish a given domain.[5]

Triangles for looking at character

The same organizer can be used to generate, recall and assimilate details of fictional characters or actual people. Fig. 2.4 illustrates the point.

- Basic identifiers. This refers to the two or three 'surface features' that create a first impression. Notice how the triangle shape offers very little space, so students have to choose their words with care.

- One unique detail. This is something that reinforces the special quality of the individual. It can be drawn from any other level. This part of the triangle is usually filled in last.

- Physical description. Again, the limitation of space requires students to be concise in their writing.

87

- Personality. We begin to see that the triangle organizer acts as a visual metaphor for the 'layeredness' of any individual. Physical appearance is influenced by the thoughts and feelings that constitute one's personality.

- Background. Similarly, one's current ongoing thoughts and feelings are brought into being by the collective experiences of one's past. We are at this moment the outcome of everything that's happened to us. This is also the level of the largely subconscious map of memory.

- Possible futures. I suggest to students that all of the levels above – how we think, what we feel, how we behave and how we appear to others – are influenced by how we imagine our personal future and what we intend to do with our lives.

Fig 2.4   Character pyramid

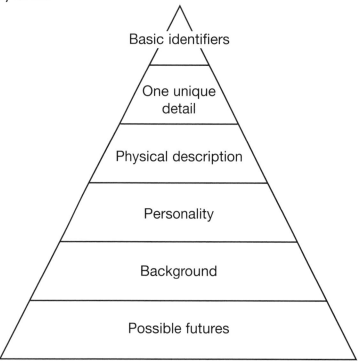

If you run this activity only a few times in a year your students will have created a resource of around one hundred quite detailed character profiles, which can be used in the following ways:

- Change one or two details in any character's past and speculate on how that might alter the makeup of the personality.

- Alter a character's outlook to the future. How might that change his or her perspective on past experiences?

- Have students sequence a number of character profiles in the order in which the students would like to meet those people.

- Put two characters together and brainstorm a possible dialogue.

- Have students select two characters who, they think, would get on well together. Explain why.

- Select two characters who would be immediately antagonistic towards one another. What might need to change in each character's makeup for this to be resolved?

- Ask students to speculate, based on their 'reading' of characters' personalities, how those characters might develop in the future. This activity, like most of the others here, tells you more about the students than the characters!

- Put characters with shared traits into groups (this is an opportunity to introduce or revisit Venn diagrams).

- Mix and match traits from two or more characters to create a new character.

Newspaper articles

Use the triangle organizer to help students understand the structure of news articles (Fig. 2.5).

Triangle organizer for reportage   **Fig 2.5**

- Headline. There is just enough room here to insert a few attention-grabbing words.

- Byline. One or two sentences sum up the overall nature of the article.

- Key ideas. Each main point is framed in a sentence. The sentences are sequenced to show the development of the story.

- Development. Further details elaborate on the main points already made.

- Opinion, quotation and conclusion. Use this space for more subjective material such as quotes from and the opinions of people featured in the article, editorial comment, and so on. Any 'rounding off' or concluding statements are also made here.

Organizing factual material

Factual material organized in this way allows information to be reviewed and remembered more reliably:

- 'Gee whiz' facts. Use an attention-grabbing idea at the peak of the triangle. This corresponds to the strong opening sentence of a story, which the author uses to tempt the reader in.

- Key points. The main ideas are written succinctly here.

- Supplementary material – further facts and so on that support the key ideas.

- Handling the information. Suggest an activity here that encourages students to engage creatively with the concepts you want them to learn. The 'What if' game works well here.

What if?

Even if this game begins with a fantastical premise, the students soon find themselves using real ideas, exploring actual themes and, often, coming up with practical solutions. They are also using the concepts and vocabulary of the area of knowledge you want them to master.

So, if the area of enquiry were to do with gravity, mass or inertia, for example, the 'what if' might be 'What if gravity switched off unexpectedly for five minutes every day?'. To keep the brainstorming and flow of ideas focused, append these three subsidiary questions to the main proposition:

- What would the world be like?

- What problems might we encounter?

- How can we solve these problems?

You can also theme the students' thinking by offering a series of subheadings such as transport, shopping, school, family life and so on. The fantastic nature of the initial 'what if' makes the game fun and the students aren't so inhibited by thinking they have to come up with 'the right answers', although useful insights and practical outcomes often arise. On subsequent occasions have the students themselves come up with their own what-if scenarios. (The science fiction writer Douglas Hill asserts that the whole field of SF is predicated on those two wonderful words 'what if'. Playing the what-if game allows students to construct more or less informed theories as they explore possible futures – where they will be spending the rest of their lives.)

Classification pyramid

The same triangle organizer can help students to visualize patterns of classification so, for instance, I put my cat Leo at the peak of the triangle and mark out the rest of the sections thus – cat, domestic pet, mammal, animal, living thing.

Structuring an argument

Use the triangle as a template for students to organize their thoughts. The initial premise or the issue to be explored is stated at the top. Subsequent sections contain key points (in favour or against), a development of those points, subsidiary material (opinions, etc.) and finally conclusions. Have students pair up, where each pair contains a student who argues for the premise and one who argues against. Have them position the triangles tip to tip to make an hourglass shape. Move it through ninety degrees to create a visual representation of a balanced argument.

Fig 2.6

Creative excursions and the eternal journey

The same shape as that in Fig. 2.6 symbolizes the most fundamental structure of narrative. Imagine the left-hand triangle as 'the hero's familiar domain'. In creative thinking terms this represents an area of knowledge we have mastered. We are authorities within our comfort zone of ideas, having created a structure of beliefs that frame our reality and perception of the world.

If a problem arises, the hero must journey to far-flung realms (the right-hand triangle). This is an unfamiliar or unknown domain. The waist of the tipped-over hourglass represents a threshold. Beyond this point we have to rely on the resources we carry with us – our ability to think flexibly and incisively, to question, to generate creative insights, to build practical re-solutions. Even though we are – as the saying goes – out of our comfort zone, our noble and heroic qualities see us through. Our resources are tested, but we return to our home realm empowered with a fresh perspective.[6]

This kind of 'learning journey' closely resembles a robust yet flexible strategy called the *creative excursion*. This is where, having encountered a problem in a familiar domain (family, or work, and so on), we look in unfamiliar places to solutions.

An example of this occurred in the 1980s. NASA, the American Space Agency, had been instructed to develop the capability to put astronauts on Mars. America had beaten the Soviets to the Moon and now wanted to repeat such political one-upmanship on a grander scale. However, spiralling costs became an increasingly contentious political issue, and eventually NASA's budget was cut, their mission now being to send cheaper, unmanned probes instead. NASA technicians now had a problem, because their energy had been invested in developing life support systems. So they took a trip to the zoo and spoke to the entomologists at the Insect House. Insects were small and tough and successful. How did they do it? The NASA people were nosy. They gathered up ideas and applied them to the domain of astro-engineering, with the result that in recent decades America's unmanned Mars exploration programmes have been largely successful.[7] Returning to the rotated hourglass shape – it's usually drawn thus to represent the basic narrative template (see Bowkett, 2003):

Mathematicians will instantly recognize the symbol for infinity. This is very appropriate, since here we have visualized the endless interconnectivity of the universe and of human endeavour. The same symbol, with a slightly different emphasis, can be used to represent the so-called Accelerated Learning Cycle, as in Fig. 2.7.

Fig 2.7   Accelerated learning cycle

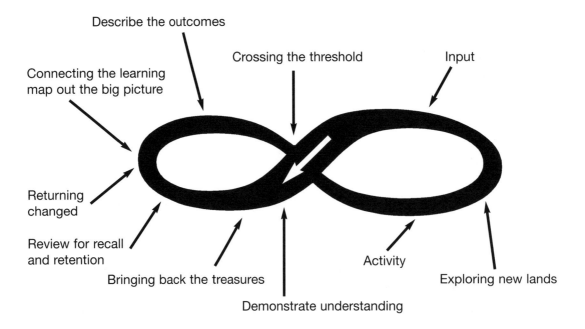

Storylines and the narrative dynamic

Stories are logical-sequential structures that have a beginning, a middle and an end, which may be illustrated as in Fig. 2.8. Imagine it as the narrative loop – ∞ – straightened out. This becomes a simple visual organizer along which information can

92

be arranged. It is also a *process metaphor* suggesting inexorable progress towards a fixed goal or resolution.

Storylines basic template   **Fig 2.8**

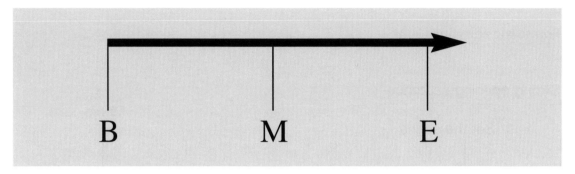

There are many ways of using the device:

- Have students annotate a storyline with key events, scenes, snippets of dialogue, vivid particularities, and so on, from stories you want them to remember. This could be in the form of a wall display with each student being given the responsibility of adding a memorable item to the line.

- The use of a story ingredient somewhere along the line prompts further enquiry. It also modifies the habit that most students have of thinking about the beginning of the narrative first. That's just one strategy. Subconsciously we're processing the entire story, so ideas can 'pop up' seemingly at random. The storyline allows students to incorporate their illuminations as they arise and building them into the emerging tale.

- Fig. 2.9 is an example of the strategy of *artful vagueness*. This is a situation where we learn something precise, or have a specific mental task to carry out, but the outcomes are still vague. In this case we know precisely where danger occurs in the story, but what kind of danger and where it could be, who might be in danger, and so on, are still vague. This simple tactic encourages questioning in the students.

Storyline with ingredient   **Fig 2.9**

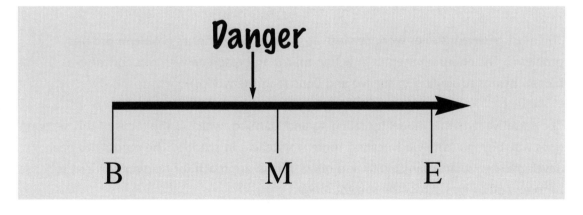

- Fig. 2.10 as a wallchart provides a constant visual reminder of points to consider when writing a robust story. Again this is artfully vague. The organizer provides a framework for further thinking but allows enough 'creative space' for students to have their own ideas.

Fig 2.10 Formulaic storyline

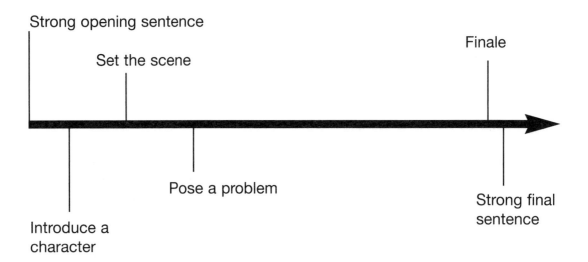

Another way of thinking about stories is not so much B–M–E but O–C–R, *orientation–complication–resolution*. Orientation refers to 'tagging' the genre, setting the scene and introducing the initial characters. More generally in terms of learning it means refreshing what we already know and reminding ourselves of the overall context of the story. The opening paragraphs that drift away into space in the Star Wars movies, for example, perform this function.

Soon after the reader 'steps through the doorway' into the fictional world – or sometimes even as this happens – a complication or problem is introduced. This may be a precursor to the story's main dilemma, or the central problem itself. Either way that narrative necessity creates drama, tension, excitement and anticipation in the reader about the adventure to come.

The most powerful stories work because at some level the hero's problems are our problems. The enduring themes in fiction mirror and resonate with our concerns as human beings struggling to survive and flourish in the world.

The narrative dynamic model for teaching and learning, which is the focus of this section, goes way beyond simply advocating more storytelling in schools. The model has been developed by Kieran Egan (1989) and offers a fresh approach for helping children to become author-ities across the subject range.[8]

Egan points out that the traditional pattern behind our pedagogy is defined by Objectives–Content–Methodology–Evaluation procedures. While not denying its usefulness, he points out that it can easily lead to a situation where students sit and passively receive facts delivered by the teacher, whose authority itself rests on how many facts *s/he* has acquired from other sources.[9] One major outcome of this approach is the development of what Edward de Bono calls 'reactive' or 'guess the right answer' thinking in students. It is a feature of classrooms where

- Questions are usually closed, rhetorical and teacher-initiated.

- 'Pre-packaged content' from outside authorities is transmitted wholesale from the teacher to the students.

- The competitive ethos is a major motivator. Such an ethos is also frequently judgemental and exclusive ('Well done David, you've got the answer right. Stephen, your answer's wrong. You must try harder next time').

- The teacher's primary concern is that the students have remembered enough 'facts'. Assessment procedures in this case are geared towards that goal.[10]

Kieran Egan's narrative dynamic model shifts the educational emphasis into the heads of the learners, which is where education takes place. The approach is dynamic because it encourages students' active engagement with ideas: it is content-*rich* but not content-*led*. It is process-led, and as Postman and Weingartner assert time and time again in their writings, *the students themselves are the process*.

Egan's model is 'narrative' because it uses the basic orientation–complication–resolution template for learning to occur. Rather than attempt to paraphrase Egan's elegant explorations of the model (in *Teaching as Storytelling*), my purpose here is simply to introduce the broad sweep of his thinking, offer an interpretation of the model that has been useful to me, and invite you to consider its potential as an alternative strategy in the classroom.

Fig. 2.11 illustrates my take on the narrative dynamic approach and how it can work. At its most basic and simplistic, the model emphasizes a problem-solving agenda to learning rather than the mere retention of facts. The orientation phase familiarizes students with the context in which the 'complication' or problem is posed. Resolving the complication is the purpose of the whole exercise. Content forms its raw material, the fuel that drives the process of enquiry; but just understanding more content or more about the content is not the primary purpose of the strategy. That happens anyway as a byproduct of the thinking that lies at the heart of the matter. Learning to think more creatively and more effectively is what it's all about. The journey is the destination.

95

Fig 2.11

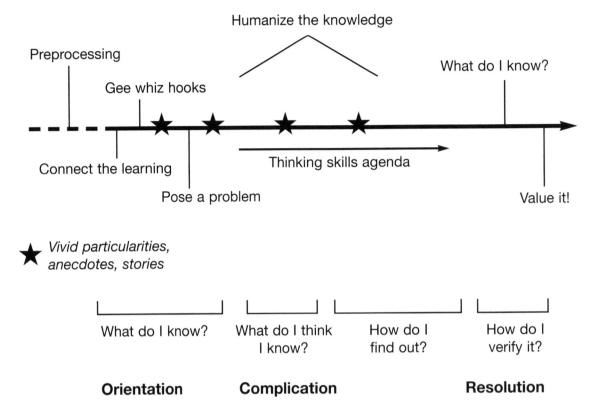

One important aspect of the model is the presence of binary or bipolar opposites, which set up conflicts and tensions in the narrative. This corresponds to Propp's identification of the hero and villain elements as eternally opposing forces. The very existence of these two elements guarantees a raft of dilemmas and problems sprinkled through the story. The narrative dynamic model uses the process of mediating between bipolar opposites as a mechanism for resolving complications. Egan also urges its use in the selection of educational content. At its most basic his 'story form' model looks like this:

- Identifying importance. What is most important about this topic? Why should it matter to the students (the 'what's in it for me?' principle)? What is affectively engaging about it – in other words, what emotional impact can it make?

- Finding binary opposites. What binary opposites help to make the topic important by creating 'dramatic tensions', dilemmas and problems?

- Establishing the narrative form. What content, and how can that content, be used as part of an 'ongoing narrative of enquiry' leading towards a resolution?

- Resolution/conclusion. How can the tension between the binary opposites best be resolved? What degree of mediation between the binary opposites constitutes a workable resolution?

- Evaluation. How can one establish how and to what extent the content of the topic has been understood?

96

The model, in common with all creative strategies, uses content to fuel learning processes. The narrative dynamic is not an add-on, but a change of emphasis that we should be able to accommodate to a greater or lesser extent within the current framework.

The scope of this section means that I can do no more than introduce the model, enthuse about it and encourage you to explore it further for yourself. The power and practicality of the approach are more than amply demonstrated by Kieran Egan himself in *Teaching as Storytelling*. But here however are a few particular examples of how 'narrative dynamic thinking' works as we prepare the ground for our students to learn:

- The teaching of comma use. Egan makes it clear that perhaps the most appropriate way to get children to master the comma is to embed the learning in some more meaningful writing activity. However, the topic serves as a useful example because it shows how the narrative dynamic approach can work on the small scale as well as with more wide-ranging areas of knowledge.

- Identifying importance. The comma is important because it contributes to a writer's individual style. That in itself is part of the greater imperative that we all feel to express ourselves powerfully and clearly. The what's-in-it-for-me element of learning about commas is that we master another small aspect of letting people know what we think and how we feel.

- Finding binary opposites. The 'hero' of expressing individuality versus the 'villain' of being unable to do so, or of being able to communicate in writing in only simple, unclear or dryly conventional ways.

- Establishing the narrative form – that is, turning the learning process into a story. A brief period of reflection will result in plenty of examples. For instance, contrasting two letters of complaint about some topical matter. One letter clearly communicates the complainant's feelings and arguments (partly through the artful use of commas) while the other is muddled, ambiguous and ineffective. The opportunity also arises here to identify other grammatical rules that can aid communication, and may lead to discussion of a more philosophical kind about what constitutes a rule/what are some different kinds of rules?/are some rules more important than others?/what if all of a sudden some rules were no longer obeyed? And so on.

Another approach would be to study comma use in favourite stories selected by the students, having them notice how commas contribute to the overall meaning and experience of the story. A third idea, which I have used myself with younger children, is to invent the evil punctuation wizard who magics away punctuation marks. To tell children to write stories that deliberately miss out punctuation is usually subversive enough to motivate them. The evil wizard's partner is the 'comma trickster' who delights in dropping commas, in, inappropriate, places. The punctuation police arrive just in time to remedy the situation.

Another suggestion is to use comma-based riddles. Consider the difference between the following.

- Charles the First walked and talked half an hour after his head was cut off.
- Charles the First walked and talked. Half an hour after, his head was cut off.

Here's one for you to try.

> Every lady in the land
> Has twenty nails upon each hand
> Five and twenty on hands and feet
> All this is true without deceit.

The resolution of the problem is the realization by the students that commas can and do make a difference. This is not something we as teachers have simply told them, and certainly we haven't just insisted that they learn the rules of comma use just because they are rules or because the curriculum demands it. The students have found out for themselves. They have learned by doing within an environment that we have engineered to ensure that that learning takes place.

This strategy, incidentally, makes use of what is known as *the principle of the controlled accident*. This is where we build our educational environment in such a way (in this case utilizing a narrative dynamic approach) that the learning we want the students to experience for themselves through their own endeavours becomes almost inevitable. Conventional test exercises for comma use form one way of evaluating mastery of the concepts. Having students teach comma use to others further demonstrates their mastery ('Show how leads to know how'). The written work they have produced on the way also acts as written evidence of understanding. Most importantly, if the students now realize that mastering comma use empowers their language, and can articulate this using their new punctuation tools, we can feel satisfied that resolution has occurred.

Fig. 2.12 offers you a chance to explore the narrative dynamic approach a little further. Its appeal to me is that it exploits the power stories have to engage students through the 'Five I's':

- *Imagination* – our wonderful ability to create mental structures beyond the here-and-now.
- *Intellectual* skills are used to actively refine and test strategies for resolution.
- *Intuition* – 'inner tuition', the ability we have to learn from ourselves and weave new meanings back into the subconscious map of reality.
- *Immersion* – stories are immersive; narratives draw us into imagined and imaginary worlds, which at their most powerful cause us to reflect upon our own lives at every level and offer opportunities for life-affirming and life-enhancing changes of perspective.

● *Interest* – the positive feedback loop of interest is swiftly established through story; interest binds the other four I's together, while they in turn generate interest in the narrative world we have created and keep us engaged.

Applying the narrative dynamic approach.

Fig 2.12

	Identifying importance	Finding binary opposites	Establishing narrative form	Resolution/ conclusion	Evaluation
America's Mars space programme	• Human curiosity ensures survival. • Psychological and spiritual implications of life elsewhere.	• The 'outward urge'/scientific endeavour. • Political one-upmanship/budget cuts.	• Letters lobbying the Senate to release funds. • 'Decision alley' technique to open debate. • Descriptive writing/art/music reflecting man's place in the universe. • Appropriate SF stories.	• Cheaper unmanned probes. • International manned missions. • Technological spinoffs to solve problems on Earth.	• Students' ability to present cases for and against manned/ unmanned missions. • Factual knowledge of spaceflight. • Ability to apply insights gained in other areas.
The ancient Egyptians					
Euclidean geometry					
The issue of introducing local car parking charges					

The ideas I have tried to bring together in these sections all have ancient roots. However swiftly the world changes around us, and however much we change, it is and always has been the case that our natural curiosity lies at the heart of our ability to survive and to flourish, not only as a species but also in our individual lives. As the writer Anatole France has said, 'The whole art of teaching is only the art of awakening the natural curiosity of the young mind for the purpose of satisfying it afterwards.' And in conclusion, to quote Ellen Parr:

The cure for boredom is curiosity. There is no cure for curiosity.

99

Notes

1   Aitchison (1995) is a thorough and highly erudite work on the topic.

2   See for instance Bettelheim (1976), *The Uses of Enchantment*. Bettelheim's book takes a now rather unfashionable Freudian slant but is useful in helping adults to become aware of the irreplaceable importance of fairy tales.

3   If you wanted to be very mischievous, reproduce Fig. 2.1 on a strip of paper and, as you curl it to bring the ends together, give it a twist to create a Möbius strip. Now tape the ends. Consider that the blank side of the strip symbolizes either what we don't know yet and/or the hidden (subconscious?) workings of the universe. Take a pencil and begin at the neck of the hourglass shape, the here-and-now. Draw a continuous line through the neurological levels and the levels of the external world. Do not lift the pencil from the paper and keep going until you return to the here-and-now. Now remove the tape and lay the strip flat. What do you notice? What have you learned?

4   The storyteller Hugh Lupton asserts that 'The ladder to the moon is based on … the custom of West African storytelling. When people gather together for a night of storytelling they will start with gossip, that is recollections from within living memory and jokes. Then will come the exploits of culture heroes. Then the magic or wonder tales. Then the myths, where the Gods intervene in human affairs. Finally as dawn is breaking you come to the stories of creation itself.' See www.spiked-magazine.co.uk/spiked8/lupton.htm.

5   For detailed applications of these ideas in the field of creative writing and the exploration of text, see Bowkett (2001, 2003).

6   Tilling (2001) is a delightful and useful exploration of the narrative template-as-learning journey.

7   Zubrin (1996) gives an excellent account of creative strategies for manned colonization of Mars.

8   Although Egan's book is subtitled *An Alternative Approach to Teaching and Curriculum in the Elementary School* my own feeling is that the model is robust enough to sustain learning at all levels of education.

9   The writer Richard Milton (1994, 1997) distinguishes two types of 'expert'. The true expert has learned through direct experience and by testing out other people's ideas. He has authority and generates his own insights. The 'hollow' expert simply reiterates the ideas of others without bringing anything fresh to the field. Milton's ideas make challenging and exciting reading.

10 Postman and Weingartner state that 'Most students suffer more from an inability to have an idea than from any other learning deficiency'. The same authors also said (heart-breakingly) that 'Children enter school as question marks and leave as full stops'.

The learning stones

A backpacker's guide to the curriculum

Tim Harding

O n the crest of a ridge, four young travellers looked out onto the landscape before them. They were plainly dressed and each carried a backpack which contained pebbles, some given to them by their family or friends, others they had gathered on previous visits.

Ann was eager to discover more. Sam just wanted to get there. Joe and Jan both stood looking: Joe thoughtful and wondering about the stones they might find today, Jan already thinking what she'd do when she got down there.

Before them lay their futures and the search for knowledge and understanding.

In front of them a great city sprawled across the plain with ten large towers dominating the skyline. From each tower it seemed as if a sector of development had spread out across the countryside, and while some suburbs spread out in orderly lines of streets, carefully planned and developed, others sprawled haphazardly.

"Look," said Ann. "The City of Words."

As the children gazed down they could see the centre of the city with its simple blocks of buildings in bright primary colours. Surrounding the centre was an area where the buildings were made of old stones containing ancient images of weird creatures. Further out from here was a ring of tall buildings painted with all kinds of characters and scenes, and finally, encircling all, the outer suburbs spread outwards with buildings where stones were placed in more logical and reasoned patterns, framed

101

with ideas, and with gardens filled with plants around them.

A network of roads ran between the different suburbs, dense near the centre of the city, but with fewer links further out. Fleets of buses and the occasional car sped along the roads.

The whole scene buzzed with activity. People like ants, scurrying and gathering – in lines, and on their own, swarming over the land. For the whole plain was strewn with stones of many shapes and colours, fashioned in various ways: plain pebbles and rare gems, hard and soft rock.

Some stones the result of evolution over thousands of years, containing fossilized remains of the dim, distant past. Others new and recently shaped by men.

Learning stones. Waiting to be gathered, and strung together by travellers on lines of thought; or sorted into meaningful patterns. Or made into structures and buildings, cemented together by beliefs.

Overhead, clouds of uncertainty, uncertain even in their own shape, shifted around the sky sometimes obscuring the sun, source of all knowledge. They scudded through the blue vastness of space pushed by the winds of influence and impulse, which veered between calm and severe urgency.

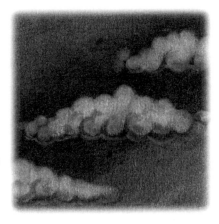

Clouds. Ever changing, hazy and unsure. Increasing in intensity until they rained their questions down onto the landscape below.

How many? How? Where? When? What? Who? Why? What with?

And as the rain fell, some of the questions broke over the stones and, in the glare of understanding, evaporated; answered, re-solved, and forgotten, until the next time they appeared, re-cycled and fresh.

And some questions trickled away among the stones, finding their way into streams and on into the river that flowed through the city. Sometimes these streams of questions were raging torrents of anxiety, sometimes they lay in deep calm pools of mystery lying unanswered. Waiting to be used by the travellers who poured them over stones to make them clearer to see. Or just waiting to join the cycle once again.

And when there was plenty of rain and the sun shone strongly with calming breezes, there was a perfect climate for learning and rainbow colours shone across the whole landscape. Among the stones, plants of value grew. Plants of many colours and textures. Large and small, deep- or shallow-rooted and be-leaved in many shapes.

The children skipped in eager anticipation along the straight road that led to the centre of the city. A long time ago, plans had been drawn, trying to rationalize and mark out areas of knowledge that lay under the clouds of questioning. And so the

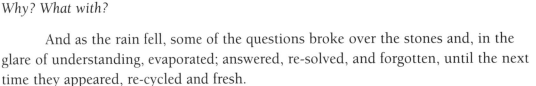

suburbs had grown, each with its own codes and conventions.

And pathways had been constructed through the landscape. A way through all the knowledge – for that's what curriculum means.

But wherever you looked there were libraries containing all kinds of writing – and so much writing, about the landscape! Manuals and commentaries, schemes and plans. Some of these gave directions for finding your way around the city. These were constantly being rewritten, routing and re-routing both the travellers and the guides.

Writings to be read, and considered, and in turn to be themselves written about. And as the travellers read and wrote, they picked up stones to put in the backpacks. It was the guides' job to help them to gather the right stones and to show them how to string the stones together using string-lines of thought made from the plants of value.

The children met their guide at the bus station. While they waited for everyone in their party to arrive, the guide checked some of the number-stones in their backpacks, to see if any one had lost the stones they'd gathered the day before.

The bus set off and they passed other groups of travellers, sorting stones and showing people what they'd made. For as the travellers gathered the stones, they often wore them as jewellery, which they could later store in their backpacks; nuggets of information linked by belief and values. The guides showed them how to make them.

There were bracelets and necklaces, belts and headbands. The bracelets took information round in a circle.

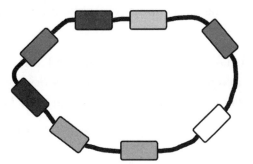

Sometimes the pieces of jewellery they made were copies of ones that had been made before, with older stones. Some travellers much preferred designing their own, although without tried and tested string-lines the stones sometimes fell off. Through experience, the guides had discovered that things went best when you used a mixture of old and new stones!

The children had been here many times before but while they recognized some of the well-trodden paths, going over them several times to make sure that everybody in their group had collected stones from there, the guides were constantly taking them into new areas. When they had first gone into the city, the guides had let them do lots of exploring themselves, but now on their visits they had to stick with the guides, only occasionally being allowed the freedom to explore.

The best guides made sure that you kept moving, knowing that some travellers were quicker at picking up stones than others, and they took you to places where there were some really good stones to pick up, in all sorts of ways. With some guides the children noticed that the buses that carried them around the city just stopped at the places they always had done.

Sometimes they'd go back to the city centre to help some of the younger travellers in the middle of the city – that was great – they often found themselves finding new stones when they did this!

Jen's favourite place was the part of the city where there were fields with dancers and actors. She loved to join in, and they would encourage travellers to try on different clothes to help them to find new stones, perhaps by looking at things in a different way.

Joe liked this place too; nearby, there were special guides to involve travellers in discussion, or you could discuss things with other travellers. As they talked he always picked up some really valuable stones.

In the next field there were travellers singing songs. The guides here held clusters of stones, tightly held together in patterns. They seemed to have an extra string-line holding them together that made them stay in your backpacks really well. Sometimes the singers would walk around the city visiting the other suburbs, giving out their extra threads – everybody had great fun when they did, but this mostly happened nearer the city centre – usually they had to stay in their own district!

Across the valley artists drew, painted and sculpted. Again some were creating their own images without looking at anyone else's, while others copied tried and tested designs.

Today their guide was taking them to a field in the Language suburb. Outside a huge building with many different departments sat some storytellers. As they spoke they were handing out stones for the children to collect in their backpacks.

Next to them sat writers, crafting poems and stories, and information.

"Writers like this used to be called wordsmiths," said the guide, "finding the very best stones – stones that matched, either at one end or the other. Finding stones that reminded them of other things and describing them as vividly as they could."

Some of the writers used metal frames to arrange their stones on before they wrote. "We're going to use some of these today," said the guide. "We're going to make stories." They all got off the bus and sat in front of her.

To start them off she needed some stones. She'd brought a bagful she'd collected earlier. Sometimes she chose the stones really carefully. Sometimes she let the travellers choose. Sometimes she found a set of stones, closed her eyes and picked one out at random. Then she'd pick another one and find a good piece of string-line to join them together.

Eyes closed, she picked out a stone. It had an image of a giant on it.

104

"There was once a dragon," she said and, closing her eyes again, picked out another three stones. To begin with she poured some water on the stones she'd chosen. It was water from the 'Where', 'When' and 'Who' pools.

When they could see them clearly, she placed them carefully in the first box of the frame. A large jug of 'What' raindrops stood ready for when the stones were moved into the next three boxes. One of the stones in the second box caused some problems, but by the fourth box these had been resolved!

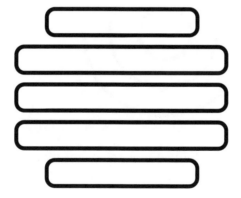

As the story finished, she strung them together, gave them a twist and made them into a story bracelet.

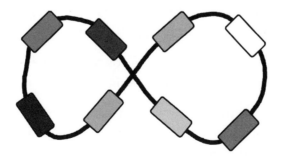

"Look how I've arranged them," she said, "and I'll put this in my backpack later, or I could write it down. That would help me to remember all the details. And other people could read about it too."

Then it was the children's turn. Sometimes they all had to use the same frame, but today they could choose a type of frame of their own.

Joe liked a rectangular frame to organize his stones in. The boxes were bound together by lines of thought.

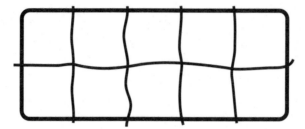

Ann liked to use a circular one where it reminded her of throwing a stone into the 'What' pond – the ripples moving out as the story unfolded.

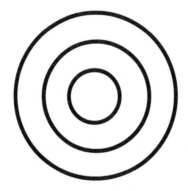

Sam entered an area that looked like an adventure playground. There was a succession of small wooden turrets and rooms connected by rope bridges and ladders. He could move large-scale pictures of stones around the inside walls of the rooms and then move along to the next room. As he moved from one to the next, he collected stones and slipped them onto his belt.

When the stories had been written they all sat on the ground and shared them with each other. As they sat looking at them some of the group were picking up stones and slipping them onto necklaces – or even putting them straight into their backpacks.

Later as they travelled on the bus, Ann watched the people they passed and noticed that some people's packs weren't working very well.

"Do you know?" said the guide, "I heard somewhere that 90 per cent – that's nearly all the stones people put in their backpacks – fall out again. Only the stones that have been really well gathered, or are held together with strong string-lines, stay in." Ann checked her backpack carefully.

106

"There's actually a small group of buildings towards the edge of the city where people study backpack design," the guide continued. She pointed to a cluster of low-profile buildings in the shadow of the towers. "Mind you, it's only a few years ago that people really started taking notice of them, but more and more people are beginning to understand how their backpacks work."

The bus pulled up in the Science quarter. Ann really liked this part of the city. They made multi-stranded necklaces which sorted different kinds of stone along separate string-lines. It helped you see the differences between the stones. There were also circular racks you could put stones in, to see groups that were the same.

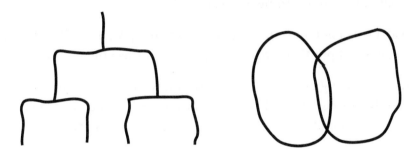

While they were there the guide wheeled out a special sort of sorting machine in front of them; this was really good for finding things out. Sam really liked using these.

The guide reminded them how to use it. "First you start off by finding some raindrops from one of the pools of questions: 'will?' or 'which?' or 'why?' or 'how?' and you pour them into the frame. Then you predict what sort of stone you think will come out of the bottom. Next you make a stone with a picture of the equipment you'll need – you may need to put some other stones in as well. You watch carefully. And finally a stone will come out of the bottom of the machine!"

They looked carefully to see if it was the colour they'd thought it would be. Sometimes when you did this, you found a new stone sticking to it. By this stage you would hope that all the water had evaporated! Sometimes more water came out than you'd put in!!

They all put copies of the green stone in their backpacks.

Jen liked the machine as well but wondered if she could design a new one; maybe one that looked a bit like they'd been using that morning.

That afternoon the bus pulled into a large unfamiliar space. It was a testing station. It looked a bit like a car wash; questions had been collected and were sprayed intensively on the travellers in the hope that they would come out brighter and shinier. And that the bus they were in would look bright and shiny too.

"Listen carefully," said a senior guide. "Your backpacks are to be evaluated. We want to see what's in them. Learning is suspended."

Sam had a collection of stones that he was really proud of. They told you how to strip engines down and put them together again. "Can I use these?" he asked.

"Oh no," said the guide. "Unfortunately you won't be needing those. This is a writing-down-only testing station. Everybody has to answer the questions. You just have to read the test carefully, and look for those stones in your packs."

"What if we're no good at writing?" said Jen.

"What if we can't find the right stones? There's so much else in there. Can't we tell you about the stones in our bag?" said Ann.

"Can't we show you some of the things we've made? I could show the stone picture of my sculpture."

"Can I use one of the Science frames?" asked Sam.

"No. That would be really good," said the guide, "but much too hard for me to do. Someone floated that sort of idea once. It sank without trace. You've got to get writing."

"Great," said Ann. She just hoped she could find the stone with the image of the story frame on it. So did the others, but they weren't sure.

And so the children jumped off the bus, their backpacks bulging with ideas, and streamed into the testing station.

Diagrammatic reasoning: theory

Tim Harding

In our multimedia, multitasking society – a world of fast-changing technology, and access to ever greater amounts of information – clarity of thought and the ability to gather, organize and process the information we receive are increasingly valuable skills. As David Hyerle wrote in 1996:

> Many are uneasy about students' capacity to access abundant information without necessarily having the tools or the time to organize, process, filter, and evaluate 'info-glut' and 'info-smog' ... our students may have the technical link to information, yet few have the mental fluency to craft information into knowledge.

The work of Hyerle and others in developing diagrammatic reasoning tools (known also as visual organizers or VLTs: visual learning tools) has enabled many teachers and their pupils to represent their thoughts graphically. At a time when teachers face continual and increasing demands to develop creativity, while simultaneously having to meet the requirements of a prescriptive curriculum, such tools are an invaluable aid not just in the processing of information but in all elements of the thinking process – including reasoning, enquiry, creative thinking and evaluation.

109

The current desire for individualism and personalized learning is also presenting new challenges. A personal vocabulary of transferable cross-curricular thinking strategies and skills is increasingly important; and graphical and diagrammatical representations of these are excellent tools with which to apply them.

There are, of course, past models for these: 'There is no thinking without an image' is a much cited saying of Aristotle; and early English literature has numerous examples of reasoning diagrams (as well as examples of the didactic form of allegory used in 'The learning stones'! – such as the medieval allegorical poem *Piers the Plowman*). James Franklin (1999) argues that

> The first successes of the Scientific Revolution were … possible because Europe had had several centuries of training with reasoning with diagrams … anything from simple family trees to complicated perspective constructions to gridded maps … the astonishingly vivid medieval visual imagination was regarded as literally full of pictures, and so a medium for scientific visualisation. It was the medium Galileo used successfully for his thought experiments.

Franklin cites as evidence the logical diagram 'Porphyry's Tree', which classifies the kinds of being, as well as numerous other examples of charts and tables.

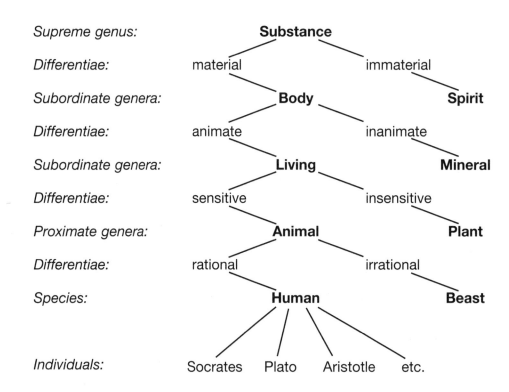

The tree of Porphyry

In both cases, medieval and modern, the key element in employing visual tools for thinking is the analysis of information and the breaking down of its component parts, which can then be manipulated and processed through graphic depiction. The concept of pieces of information as items of thought which can be sorted and organized into meaningful patterns allows us to visualize this organization, and leads to the different types of visual learning tools.

The reconstruction of these visual learning tools into desired formats can then be achieved. It is the conversion of the abstract into the concrete through visualization which enables us to demonstrate and teach thinking processes and subsequently re-inform the abstract. 'The learning stones' is based on this metaphor.

Combined with the ability to generate information, whether through random selection, reasoned choice or prescription, the provision of visual structures and templates is a valuable organizational tool for pupils of all ages. And if we are to equip our pupils with such skills and strategies, this is a process which needs to be embraced across all Key Stages and in a way which is completely transferable across subject areas, with pupils able to draw on their experiences in order to select suitable graphic models, and able to transfer material easily from one to another.

The introduction of visual learning tools begins in the concrete sorting, matching and sequencing exercises of the Foundation Stage curriculum. Providing models which link these both to the diagrammatic visual tools of older pupils and to writing frames is a vital step. For example, the practical sequencing of a set of illustrations which tell a well-known story can lead directly to the type of narrative structure diagram shown in 'The learning stones'. This exercise will identify the component parts of a story – introduction/setting – dilemma – action – confrontation – resolution/conclusion. The diagram can be filled in with age-appropriate language, using either single words or phrases. These can form the planning basis for sentences or paragraphs for pupils in the later stages of KS1 and above. The assimilation of such a diagrammatic model for stories will be a useful planning tool for pupils throughout their education.

Hyerle writes that 'students must be creative users of visual tools. These should not just be graphics to fill in – there needs to be a purpose as well as a particular context so that the tools lead to a final product.' The use of the narrative structure diagram fulfils these criteria: it is a visual analysis tool which can lead a pupil from the non-verbal visual (illustrations), through analysis and organization, to a verbal or visual product. Technology allows us to use the diagram as an increasingly interactive tool in the classroom, made even more so through tactile use of whiteboards by pupils: 'thoughts' and key information can be manually organized in a way which actively involves the pupils. It can also be used as a valuable teaching tool in the sequential 'revealing' of parts of a diagram as a method of leading and directing classroom discussions. The transfer of information into computer modelling programs can be equally valuable.

111

However, much of what we teach is still two-dimensional in many ways, including diagrams on paper. One of the most popular forms of visual learning tools used in the classroom is the mind map, an excellent device for recording and communicating ideas in a 'big picture', holistic way. It can demonstrate the links and relationships between items or concepts, and is a very useful tool in the collation of information. However, a problem that many pupils find with diagrams such as mind-maps is that often these are used as a precursor to presenting the information in a written form (usually prose). The subsequent organization and ordering of the content into a logical and sequential order can be very difficult.

Nevertheless, there is a further past model that can extend our teaching of thinking skills. If they could afford it (nothing changes), medieval thinkers would use a three-dimensional model to represent choice. Franklin comments, 'It can at least be said that the medieval and Renaissance mind would have regarded a complex building that did not represent the zodiac, or the virtues, or the macrocosm, or all of these at once, as a crying waste of representational possibilities.' He continues:

> Space is three-dimensional. Diagrams can use all three dimensions … the cycles of frescos are a diagram of the history of the universe, also of the life of Christ, also of the pilgrimage of the individual soul. The cycles end at the back wall, on reaching which one is intended to impose a logical IF–THEN–ELSE structure: IF the soul chooses virtue, THEN go to the top part of the wall, and view the delights of paradise; ELSE …

Three-dimensional modelling can help us to organize our thoughts logically and chronologically and thus consider more than one aspect at once. In order to facilitate this we must explore further (bearing in mind the development of the new generation of 'screenagers') the capabilities of technology. Graphical thinking skills programs in information technology are partly meeting this need, but many of these tend still to be two-dimensional.

Recently I took my laptop computer into an early years classroom. On showing a small group of children a picture of the three little pigs, with the inferential clue of a bushy tail protruding from a bush, I asked the children what they thought it might be. 'I think it's the big bad wolf,' said a four year old boy. 'Click on it quick and we'll find out.' This expectation of the layering of information – accessed by the click of a mouse – is now taken for granted by the youngest children, and most children of school age are thoroughly familiar with complex adventure games and narrative journeys through a succession of screen situations involving choice and decision. Recent developments in the discrete teaching of thinking skills using digital technology through such narrative formats are to be welcomed as an enhancement to the more familiar 'pencil and paper' visual tools which support powerful and effective thinking.

Through programs using two-dimensional visual learning tools that lead to further screens through hyperlinks we can extend thinking skills further, and provide access to added layers of knowledge with more detailed information, including sounds and moving images. The example of the narrative structure-planning diagram described above can be made even more effective through the use of linked screens. It also provides a rational tool for organizing the information available.

Logical thought needs frameworks and patterns. Visual diagrams provide us with templates for these. The integration of such diagrams with the technological options now available to us can be applied to classroom planning and practice, across the curriculum. Combined, they give us the facility to take our classroom thinking into the third dimension.

Diagrammatic reasoning: practice

Tim Harding

The processing of information begins in the Early Years classroom where visual modelling is an integral part of the classroom experience. For example, concrete objects are often sorted by placing two overlapping hoops on the ground – a practical precursor to the written Venn diagram. Indeed many visual learning tools are tacitly used in Early Years education – often without their recognition as such.

It is important to familiarize pupils with as many different forms as possible at this stage, enabling them to develop a vocabulary of Visual Learning Tools. This then creates the capability for pupils to select an appropriate form for the task in hand as they progress through the Key Stages of education. Teachers at the later Key Stages need to be aware of earlier experiences and relate them to the acquisition of more complex visual learning tools.

Visual learning tools come in many forms and can be classified in a number of ways. They can be a resource for organizing subject matter either creatively or following logical patterns, for example:

Sorting	Venn diagram
	Sorting tree
	Carroll diagram
	Bar chart
	Classification grid
	Matching games (pairs, etc.)

Logical sequencing (flow charts)

Fictional	Storylinks
	Storyboard
	Story planning sheet
	Storyweb
Non-fictional	Mind maps
	Process chains
	Events sequence chains (cause and effect)
	Cycles
	Non-fiction writing plans (instructions, explanations, reports, discussions, etc.)
	Character profiles
	Mathematical operations

Visual learning tools can be applied across the curriculum; the information to be processed can be in the form of images, words or phrases. This content can be generated in a number of ways either by the teacher or by pupils. For sorting tasks for example, a set number of pieces of information can be given. With creative work, content can often be created from the children's own imaginations and ideas.

For a more structured approach to creativity, ideas can be acquired 'randomly' from pre-selected data. Random selection methods can include:

- using a set of cards or words
- drawing cards from a 'bag of ideas'
- using a spinner
- using a dice to select ideas from a co-ordinates grid.

Allowing children to choose from an existing 'pool' of ideas supports the creative process. The number of items of information should be age and subject appropriate.

Activities can be modelled on whiteboards for use by the whole class in discussion/whole-class activities (for example, drama) and then carried out either on prepared cards, as pencil and paper activities, or on computers.

The following specific examples from the groups shown above give an indication of how diagrammatic and visual modelling processes can be revitalized throughout the Key Stages.

Sorting

Venn diagrams

The visualization of the sorting process can be engaged through the use of Venn diagrams. As already mentioned, a common sorting practice in an early years classroom is to place two overlapping hoops on a classroom floor. Children are encouraged to sort solid objects by placing them in the correct hoop or in the overlapping space in the case of uncertainty or dual purpose.

This directly translates into overlapping circles on paper with representations of objects in the circles. For example:

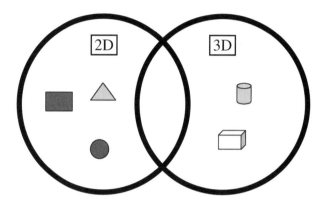

The transition to two-dimensional is complete when the Venn diagram contains numbers or words and becomes essentially a mathematical tool. However, the Venn diagram can usefully be reinvigorated as a visual learning tool for all areas of the curriculum, building on the concepts mastered earlier. Computer program can facilitate this process, for example by using drag-and-drop functions to sort pictures of objects into diagrammatic models such as Venn diagrams. (Used as part of the history curriculum, for example, the objects could be pictures of historical artefacts such as domestic items, which can be sorted according to a variety of criteria.)

Logical sequencing

Fictional: story planning

When story planning, a five-part story grid can be a useful diagrammatic tool

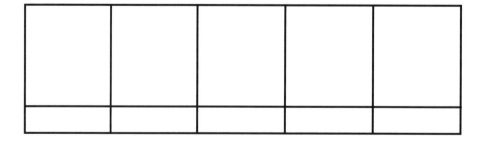

This can be enhanced at different levels to progress through the Key Stages. In Early Years and KS1 classes this process can begin with a simple sequencing of five pictures. This can progress to the addition of key words to accompany each picture and then extend to adding words connected with plot. Another variant would be the addition of speech. Finally, the model can be used as a basis for verbal and, eventually, written re-tellings of the story.

Older children (KS2) can use the model as a framework for a five paragraph story. The following five elements incorporated into the framework can help to reinforce the concept of narrative structure:

1 Setting

2 Problem or dilemma

3 Action 1 – development

4 Action 2 – development

5 Action 3 – confrontation, resolution and conclusion

The transition is therefore made to the prose writing of a story. Other forms of writing could be structured in the same way.

Non-fictional

The 'process machine'

The 'process machine' will be familiar to many KS2 children from maths lessons, where it is often presented as a 'function machine'. Numbers are entered and then processed – in this case, for example, multiplied by 2:

In later years this can be developed as a useful visual learning tool. The visual concept of entering information into a machine that can process, manipulate and change it is very vivid. For example this can be developed and related to the scientific process. It can also help to clarify understanding of predicted or known reactions in further science work, as shown below, which models exothermic reactions.

Into the third dimension

In progessing to a third dimension of visual learning tools, an obvious development is the use of computer hyperlinks, where the relating of one screen to another allows for a practical association and progression of thoughts. Encourage students to plan and use such links both within and between programs.

Enter by small rivers

Roy Leighton

An imaginary letter to Thomas Aquinas from his brother John

My most beloved and venerable brother Thomas,

I write out of desperation, loneliness and confusion. My time here at the monastery is proving to be suffering beyond all endurance. I am frustrated, disgraced and confused to levels greater than all that I had ever imagined and feared. Never in my previous incarnation as a soldier have I met such challenges.

We spend our days in exhausting physical servitude to the Lord our God in the form of tending to the farm, cleaning all areas of the monastery and in never-ending prayer and recitation and study of Holy works (much of yours among the number). While the physical toil means little to me the learning and scribing is a greater challenge. My failings in this area seem to invite scorn and ridicule from those around me.

Being a novice seems to be an excuse for my seniors to provide tasks and duties of such challenge and humiliation that it would test a saint. I have to fight my instinct to react in anger and violence to their taunts and laughter. Maybe this is their reasoning? That through the challenges I face daily I am purified and become that much closer to God? Is it possible that their love and desire for my salvation is driving their cruelty towards me?

The times of quiet reflection and love that drew me to the vocation of monk are still strong, but are less likely to be found within the austere setting of the great chapel.

Even as I write this I feel the burden of sin upon me – but I must speak freely to you, my brother, least I explode in madness and despair. I have suffered in this Holy prison for more than nine months and can no longer keep my thoughts and needs silent.

Forgive me if what I say is contrary to some dusty law decreed by some dead Pope at some point in the past but I am finding that this palace of learning and devotion is making me stupid and destroying my faith. The place of stillness and being in the presence of God is seldom amid the incense and chanting of the Abbey but more often in the gardens and fields of the grounds. In the smallest of tasks, such as seed planting and the removal of dead leaves and flower heads, is where I feel his presence most. Is this an indication that I am not suited to this life? Am I to become like the unkempt and comical Brother Francis whose tasks of maintaining the garden I have taken on  since his death? He was a figure of humour and ridicule among the brothers. I have learned (one of the few things that I have been able to learn) that Brother Francis only kept his place in the order because he was hard-working and did not object to manual labour as many of the brothers here do.

I am more suited to the dirt and grime of a battlefield. The challenges and demands of a military life are nothing to me – but this life of learning is a battle I fear I may lose. I am sincere in my calling – that my hand should move from violence and blood to prayer and study – but I now feel that I am on the point of defeat and seek help. I am turning to you, Thomas, as there seems no one else who might bring light to the darkness that now surrounds me. Not the Prior, not my fellow brothers, and not, it would seem, God.

I look to find my path to God in austere prayer on cold church floors but find his breath in the wind, and his splendour in the simplicity of things that grow and provide beauty to the eye and food for the belly. Is this a sin? Not to see God where all around seem to glory in his presence but rather to sense his love and be embraced by his power while feeding swine and covered in filth? Am I as hopeless as a man as I was as a boy?

Should we even seek to learn and change if God has already predetermined our failure? Could it be that Holy War is where I should place my talents to bring Glory to God? Is it vanity for me to seek to move from a lowly place of slaughter and abuse to take action to elevate my mind and my soul? Indeed, to become more glorious than God intended may be a form of blasphemy and an offence to God himself. Should I just stay dull and keep God happy?

I hope that my failings in areas of my calling do not give the Prior the reasons he needs to deny my rise from novice to monk. He often makes reference to your time here as one of 'divine learning' and how you could 'illuminate the darkness of ignorance for all that were blessed to share time with you'.

When I seek to contribute to the discussion and debates, as I know you did, little encouragement is made to draw forth the truth I seek to express. I lack the words. Or rather, the words and thoughts that are clear in the silence and stillness that flood me when I am alone and surrounded by natural things abandon me when under the scrutiny of others. When I most need to share the insights and visions that I know I possess I am left standing dumbfounded and babbling.

Only today, having sought to comment on one of your works about how the soul is linked directly to the mind of God, Brother Matthew described my speed of speech and slowness of wit as 'an out of control hay-wagon that has passion and drama but no direction or control'. This brought much merriment from the other brothers.

Having others find you as nothing more that a source of humour is as damaging for the soul as a whip is to the body. These are meant to be learned men, but while they can recite from memory the works of all the Saints and Popes they fail to see the suffering their comments can have on the hearts and minds of the young.

When I arrived nine months ago, I imagined the joy of living a life with enlightened men of love and truth. I am coming to the realization that the learning that is valued is that which can be seen and shown and the learning that is felt and known through the soul is belittled, disregarded and degraded. Unless I learn the things they know then I must be a lesser man than they. Surely having new knowledge and different views is what is required of a place of learning, not the perpetuation of things that have been and the reinforcement that the world is 'thus'? As I write this, my beloved and most venerable brother, I feel the enormity of difference within me and I weep.

In studies with my fellow acolytes it is as if I catch the same knowledge as they but, only a few hours later, lack the capacity to return the knowledge to the brother that imparted it. This failure to show commitment to memory is frustrating to all and Brother Ignatius shows this with loud ranting and foul speech which only seems to have a worsening effect on my ability to recall. If I studied less would this allow space in my mind for the few key things I need to complete my training? Am I overwhelming my soul by seeking to feed it that which it has no ability or capacity to absorb? Are there some that are capable (such as yourself) and others that are slow and will never acquire learning no matter how long and how hard they try?

I remember that you were always talking of discovering truth that is higher and wider and deeper. I am trying to follow your beloved example and choosing the most challenging books in the library. I do this in the hope that the hugeness of their content will stretch the smallness of my mind. After only a brief time of reading these works I feel my stupidity is only reinforced, since I am barely able to understand the words let alone the complexity of the ideas. But I will persevere until I break through this cloud of unknowing or am absorbed so totally by my ignorance that I realize that the jewel of knowing will never be mine. I am already close to this realization and am drafting letters to my former commanders in the army to seek a commission to war. Having so profoundly failed as a studious disciple of Christ then the alternative is to be a soldier for him. I do not wish to do this, and would entreat you, Thomas, to write to me quickly with a key to unlock the vault of learning and memory. I know I can, given more favourable circumstances, think and obtain insights. You know this too.

You may remember it was I that first mooted the concept of the self and the world being as one. Do you recall? It was during the time when our beloved mother insisted that you reside with her and not follow the calling you desperately yearned for. I was there as both brother and guard to make sure you did not depart. I was young and had just completed my military training and was vain and full of bluster and the pomposity of youth.

We were both walking in the vineyard and were laughing and happy. You were talking of the miracle of transforming the grape to wine and a thought sprang from me that, like unseen branches, we were linked to the earth, and therefore to the vine. These connections were infinite and eternal, reaching beyond self and outward through the earth and others to touch God himself. Do you recall that moment of joy? You encouraged my ramblings and asked me to speak more about the thing that I could feel instinctively. You helped me take the feeling and form it into words. You later put this idea down in writing but it was my idea. Say that you remember, dear brother! I do not request this of you to lay claim to the works that you have built on the passing remark of a boy soldier in a vineyard. I merely seek confirmation that I am not, as Brother Ignatius believes me to be, 'as a block of wood when it comes to learning, understanding and capacity to recall'.

If I can speak and think in one place why, when transferred to another place, do my mind and thinking lose their rigour and capacity? Thomas, help me, I pray you. I do not believe that I can sustain this Holy existence. Is God showing me that learning of this nature and this place is not for me and I should return to the life of a gentleman soldier and take on a more predestined path? Or is this the challenge, that I should transform this aspect of my being, and in changing my stupidity in learning I may become more enlightened in my understanding of God, his ways and my purpose?

I fight the jealousy in my nature that makes me resent your obvious gifts, but it seems that the expectation of all was that I would be at least competent in basic studies and recitation – and it is here that I fail the most! I am desperate, dear brother, for you to furnish me with some insight, some tool that would prevent the learning I most need and yearn from slipping out of my memory as sand is pulled unstoppably to the lower chamber of an hourglass.

I do my best to please the other brothers, and only Brother Theodore, who seems to like nothing more than to find fault and blame in all and everything except himself and his actions, spends time with me. I am without friends and lacking the capacity to live this life. Help me, Thomas, lest I sink into the blackness and despair of stupidity and abandonment.

I desire above all to do my duty and to serve my God, which at this time seems to be far off and unobtainable. Can you provide me with some guidance if not to evolve then at least to endure?

Write soon with words of hope,

Respectfully, your obedient and loving brother,

John

A real letter from Thomas Aquinas to his brother John

Because you have asked me, my brother John, most dear to me in Christ, how to set about acquiring the treasure of knowledge, this is the advice I pass on to you: that you should choose to enter by the small rivers, and not go right away into the sea, because you should move from easy things to difficult things.

Such is therefore my advice on your way of life:

I suggest you be slow to speak, and slow to go to the room where people chat.

Embrace purity of conscience; do not stop making time for prayer.

Love to be in your room frequently, if you wish to be led to the wine cellar.

Show yourself to be likable to all, or at least try; but do not show yourself as too familiar with anyone; because too much familiarity breeds contempt and will slow you in your studies; and don't get involved in any way in the deeds and words of worldly people.

Above all, avoid idle conversation; do not forget to follow the steps of holy and approved men.

Never mind who says what, but commit to memory what is said that is true: work to understand what you read, and make yourself sure of doubtful points.

Put whatever you can into the cupboard of your mind as if you were trying to fill a cup.

Seek not the things that are higher than you.

Follow the steps of blessed Dominic, who produced useful and marvellous shoots, flowers and fruits in the vineyard of the Lord of Hosts for as long as life was his companion.

If you follow these things, you will attain to whatever you desire.

Farewell,

Thomas

Thomas Aquinas and the art of memory

Roy Leighton

Et sunt quatuor per quae homo proficit in bene memorando
And there are four things by which a man makes progress in remembering well

St Thomas Aquinas was driven to help create systems for learning for both himself and his fellow brothers because documents and books took years to produce and there was a practical need for monks and priests to absorb knowledge, facts, figures, biblical passages and papal decrees quickly and effectively.

It is hard now to imagine the continual life of study that Aquinas and his fellows engaged in. They were, for all intents and purposes, the encyclopedias for the church, the state and the aristocracy. They were the literate ones and did not confine their learning to theology. Languages, art, literature, astronomy, astrology and science in its widest forms were all on the curriculum for those wanting to engage in the monastic life. Johan

Gutenberg would not invent the printing press until halfway through the fifteenth century, which meant that Thomas, who lived between 1224 and 1274, had to use other means for assisting learning and recall.

Thomas's model stands up to the rigours of time because it was based on solid reasoning, creative thinking and practical results. Recent breakthroughs in scientific understanding, particularly in the areas of neuroscience, support his four fundamental keys for memory.

In arguably his most influential work, *Summa Theologica*, Thomas gives a guide to those that wish to develop a strong and lasting memory. In this age of the internet, getting information has never been easier or more immediate. However, keeping that knowledge and accessing it at will seems to be a dying art. If we have the knowledge at our fingertips via computer then why hold it all in our head?

According to the 'Darwinian brain theory' the brain is designed to focus more on survival rather than the mere accumulation of information. If something is not going to help our survival then what is the point of giving it brain space? Brain space that is, from a neurological perspective, to all practical purposes infinite. No one has ever reached the point of saying "Well, that's all my brain potential filled". No computer yet invented even comes close to the human brain in complexity and capacity.

You and your brain are reading this section with this question in mind: "And how will my reading this assist my evolution?" Good question, and quite right too! Aquinas, through his observations and insight, gleaned this point clearly, and encourages the reader to question and seek clarity of uncertain points if learning is going to be effective.

As preface to these four points made in *Summa Theologica* Thomas reminds his readers that they need to manage their emotional response to the person imparting the knowledge and not allow personal timidity to stand in the way of questioning areas of uncertainty and doubt that may get in the way of understanding:

> Never mind who says what, but commit to memory what is said that is true: work to understand what you read, and make yourself sure of doubtful points. Put whatever you can into the cupboard of your mind as if you were trying to fill a cup.

Aquinas makes the important point that we should focus on the message and not the messenger: 'Never mind who says what…'. However, our brain is constantly assessing situations to see if we need to engage or listen (back to the Darwinian brain theory). If the person delivering the learning and the person receiving it have not formed an emotional relationship of trust then learning is unlikely. If we are judging negatively the person we are delivering to or the person doing the delivery then we are not even over the first fence, because our emotional state is not open. If the learning is one-way and a child does not feel comfortable enough to ask questions to make themselves 'sure of doubtful points' then they may be quiet, but they are unlikely to learn.

A friend and colleague of mine, Dr Andrew Curran, one of the leading figures in the world of peadiatric neuroscience, has some very straightforward advice on creating the right emotional state for learning: 'You cannot get your fucking brain to work if your fucking heart is not.' We have to be in a state where we feel 'capable and lovable' to learn.

The anxiety that blocks learning for children does not stop at adulthood. We just create more strategies to deal with or deny it. If we lack the confidence to say we do not know and instead suffer in silence because we do not want the wrath, humiliation or embarrassment of revealing our ignorance, then, as Aquinas points out, we remain ignorant. If we are reluctant to question because we do not feel comfortable with how the message is delivered then that state of affairs must be addressed.

Oh, and for those of you who just read the earlier passage and responded defensively to its language, I apologize. I just wanted to highlight Aquinas' message in a practical way. Because the information was delivered to you in a way that might not fit in with either your values or your preferred learning style then it is a natural neural response to seek safety and security. When we encounter anything we perceive as a threat to our thinking or our world our brain's response is to fire up a warning shot in the form of chemicals to tell us to fight, run, freeze or flock (be with people who see the world as we do and who will reassure us that it is okay). So, ideas that are not congruent with one's preferred learning style can often be perceived, and instinctively reacted to, as a 'threat'. Therefore, when a student is having learning delivered in a way that does not fit his learning preference, and no effort is made by the educator to discover this natural preference, the survival state will kick in with its consequent behavioural challenges.

While Thomas did not know the neurological causes, he did observe the effects and wanted to reassure his readers that they should not let their emotions disrupt their learning. It is quite likely that you need to re-read the last two paragraphs if the profane language triggered off your neurological defence mechanism. I promise, no more bad language. I simply wanted to make a point and not just give a bit of theory. And although Dr A. Curran is the most foul-mouthed paediatric neurologist I know, he does make a valid point.

Should you be reading this thinking that all this talk of feelings and love is moving into the realms of the emotional and/or creative, and is not for those of a serious academic persuasion, then we should return to Aquinas and consider his first and primary advice – that imagination and creativity are the starting points for learning:

> The first of these things is that he should find certain things [or mental images] that match the things he wants to remember, but this should not be at all usual:

because we marvel more at things which are unusual, and the soul is held by such things more and with greater force; whence it happens that we remember more those things that we see in childhood.

Therefore the devising of such likenesses and images is necessary, because simple and spiritual intentions fall out of the soul very easily if they are not linked to some physical likenesses: because human cognition is more powerful with regard to sensible things.

Hence the [faculty of] memory is placed in the sensitive part [of the soul].

Research on brain-compatible learning shows that the more emotionally aroused the brain is, the more memorable the learning will be. Daniel Goleman, author of the staggeringly insightful book *Emotional Intelligence* (1996), explains that we remember more when chemicals generated in the brain via a gland called the amygdala are excreted into the brain and the rest of the body via the nervous system:

The more intense the amygdale arousal, the stronger the imprint; the experiences that scare or thrill us the most in life are among our most indelible memories. This means that, in effect, the brain has two memory systems, one for the ordinary facts and one for the emotionally charged ones.

Aquinas, without understanding the complex mechanics, was aware of the process and encouraged students to create an emotional intensity around the learning.

So, stage one is a bit of whole-brain thinking but in order to further enhance the memory we need to bring a bit of order into the equation:

Second, it is necessary that a man should arrange in an orderly way the things that he wishes to hold by memory under his consideration, so that from one remembered thing he may progress easily to another.

As someone who works well with order and structure I like this point. The brain responds well when it has pathways to travel. The thoughts that speed around the brain travel through numerous routes and pathways. The more these pathways are used, the stronger the links.

Depending on an individual's learning preference the pathway or structure will differ from one person to another. For visual learners the preference might be mind mapping, picture notes or colour coding, to name but a few. For auditory learners, audio notes, talking things through regularly, vocal repetition and music would help. For kinesthetic/tactile learners the preferred route might be moving, sticking notes around a room, construction, image making or building. Ideally, and to reinforce the whole brain approach, then all learning styles should be included as this generates multiple links and connections.

128

Aquinas then goes on to reinforce the earlier point about the learner feeling capable and lovable and that the information is not only relevant to what they are undertaking but interesting and something they feel passionate about:

> Third, a man should apply interest and emotional energy to the things he wants to remember: because the more deeply something is impressed upon the soul, the less does it drop out of the soul.

Aquinas is highlighting the necessity to make learning relevant and, dare I say it, fun. If we do not see the point of what is being taught and it is delivered in a boring, unexciting and predictable way, then the brain cannot learn. The student might want to learn, but if the environment does not provide the conditions for learning to take place then it can become an actual block to learning. If this experience is repeated day after day, week after week, year after year, then the mental programming undergone by the child leads him or her to perceive that s/he is stupid and that learning is not something for him or her. This can take much effort and time to redress. In most cases it never is redressed, and people spend their adult lives believing themselves to be stupid when, in fact, they are not.

Aquinas is not saying that the rational should be abandoned in favour of the creative. We cannot make such a simplistic and stark distinction between rational and creative. The processes and outcomes of creativity are usually rational in the sense of being amenable to reason – though they are not always 'linear-sequential'. Similarly, rationality in terms of logical reasoning often benefits from creative 'out of the blue' insight.

Rather, Aquinas is seeking to show that unless we challenge ourselves in using all facets of our brain then we reinforce an approach that is comfortable for us at that stage in our intellectual and emotional maturity. Surely learning is about sparking up areas of the brain that are dormant, waiting for the right stimulation in order to come alive. Back to Goleman:

> In a sense we have two brains, two minds – and two different kinds of intelligence: rational and emotional. How we do in life is determined by both – it is not just I.Q. but emotional intelligence that matters. Indeed, intellect cannot work at its best without emotional intelligence. Ordinarily the complementarity of limbic system and neocortex, amygdale and prefrontal lobes, means each is a full partner in mental life. When these partners interact well, emotional intelligence rises – as does intellectual ability.

Aquinas, as Goleman states, is seeking to raise the intellectual capacity of the learner by bringing in a balance between the creative and the logical, structure and emotion. Many of us actually accomplish this approach by preferring to work in the way that is most comfortable, rather than the way that is most effective. That is not to say that a comfortable, favoured style cannot also be the most effective in some cases. The point here is that if we allow our comfort to close us to new ways of thinking and doing then

129

we may never experience an alternative, potentially more effective, more comfortable and, as well, more exciting approach.

This re-thinking and re-acting is what we are asking our children to do every day. This capacity to review, unlearn, relearn and re-do is also what makes a mature adult. However, and here's the rub, if we have been educated to 'know' rather than 'learn' we feel uncomfortable to re-think and recognize when new information makes our current understanding redundant. We all have a tendency to hold on to a view of the world as we want it to be, and not, necessarily, as it is. If we, as educators and parents, are not open to re-think and re-do, then why should we expect our children to engage with that which we have become closed to?

It is this constant repetition of the message that 'you can' or 'you cannot' that contributes to the formation of our characters, and challenging this is the final key to sustained and easily accessible memory. Aquinas commences this fourth point by quoting from an earlier work from Tullius (now known to us better as Cicero):

> Hence Tullius also says, in his Rhetoric (book 3, ch. 19), that meditations keep memory: because, as it says in the same book: custom or habit is like nature: hence the things that we understand many times we also recall quickly, as if moving from one thing to another in some sort of natural order.

If we are to embed learning we need to recognize that to just learn it once is not enough. The synaptic spark that occurs when we make learning really engaging will not be sustained unless we have the chance to review.

For those of you who are primary teachers or accelerated learning teachers across the Key Stages this model may have more resonance than for some in secondary education where a multiple intelligence curriculum is still the stuff of training days and not accepted classroom practice. There are many examples of excellent post-primary practice. However, it is true to say that the dynamic balance between process, creativity and emotional learning evident in primary school has, in British secondary education, become driven by too much of point two: it has become over-structured.

If education is really to matter to each and every child then structures need to be more in line with what is happening at Reception and primary level. The complexity of working that is constantly making the environment creative, within a flexible, changing structure where children's curiosity and questioning is encouraged and not suppressed and where review is little and often, absolutely reflects Aquinas' model for optimum learning and memory.

Finally, you will note that Aquinas does not once state that there are those who are 'clever' and those who are 'stupid'. His belief was that through personal challenge we

130

gain understanding of ourselves and bring salvation to the soul, regardless of who we are and from whence we came. Although he had the mission and passion to draw people closer to a state of grace through understanding their relationship with God, this path was unlikely to unfold unless the person walking it had not only the capacity to learn but also to review their learning and change their thinking in the light of new and reasoned agreement. This message has echoed throughout the centuries; it is best summed up by the words of Alvin Toffler, in *Future Shock* (1972):

> The illiterate of the 21st century will not be those who cannot read or write, but those who cannot learn, unlearn and relearn.

Now that we are in the twenty-first century it is clear that Aquinas and others have been speaking a truth that we would do well to heed, unless of course we do not like the message or the messenger. In either case we would not be over the first hurdle as laid out be Aquinas himself:

> Never mind who says what, but commit to memory what is said that is true.

Aquinas' message is as true today as it has ever been, and poses us this question. Do we individually and organizationally have the vision, passion and humility to challenge what we know does not work and replace it with what, so obviously, does?

Memory skills exercises

Roy Leighton

In this final section I am providing eight practical memory aids to assist all intelligence types, drawing from the science of multiple intelligences as set out by Howard Gardner (1993). Once students have had the chance to explore learning using all intelligences they can then build on learning from a basis of individual strength and preference. When they feel more confident in their capacity as learners because they are getting results using a learning preference they will be more ready and able to develop their other untapped intelligences and abilities throughout their lives.

Whatever 'intelligence' you or your students choose to use you need to keep in mind the conditions that need to be in place for the brain to work. Aquinas was clear that you need structure, emotional engagement, imagination and review for memory to be lasting. The following exercises have been set out in such a way to support this principle. I have created a simple but effective tool for review called 'The Leighton Learning Matrix', based on the work of Dr Herman Ebbinghaus (1850–1909) and his 'Curve of Forgetting'.

As a further key to hold on to as you work through the exercise sheets remember that the brain was designed not to learn but to survive. The brain will prioritize by meaning, value and relevance as well as challenge, fun and interest. Introduce the acronym R.I.N.G. to students to help them remember the four conditions for sparking up the brain:

R   *Relevant* – if an individual does not see how some new learning can assist their growth, survival or gain then the brain will find the learning hard to engage with and almost impossible to recall.

132

I   *Interesting* – if you are not interested in learning or what is being presented you will not invest energy in engaging with or recalling it.

N   *Naughty* – if something is rude, cheeky, rule-breaking or challenging then we remember. When we have an emotional and multisensory stimulating experience then the brain fires up. Advertising agencies use this technique all the time.

G   *Giggle* – if it is fun or makes you laugh you are more likely to remember – partly because it is entertaining, but also because positive chemicals are helping strengthen the neural connections in the brain.

One out of four of the above conditions and you will get the brain awake and learning. If none of these are present in any learning environment then no learning will take place. If all four R.I.N.G. conditions are present the experience will be unforgettable. Think about it. When was the last time that you had a relevant, interesting, naughty, fun experience? Precisely!

The exercises have been written with Key Stage 3 and 4 students in mind. The exercises can be used individually but have been set out to be delivered as part of a scheme of work over an eight-week period and should be delivered in order. The final task is for students to present their learning to a group (interpersonal). When working with younger children (KS2) teachers can use the exercise sheets, with a little tweaking, as a basis for developing their own games and exercises.

Finally, these exercises require a balance between creativity, structure and consistent effort. The brain, like any other muscle, requires regular exercises to grow and remain fit. This process is more about creative effort, structure and discipline than natural gifts and reinforces Edison's statement that genius is 1 per cent inspiration and 99 per cent perspiration.

1 Interpersonal or social memory

Interpersonal learners are 'people-persons'. They enjoy being around other people, like connecting and talking, have many friends and engage in social activities. They can develop genuine empathy for the feelings of others. They learn best by relating, sharing and participating in co-operative group environments. The best salespeople, consultants, community organizers, counsellors and teachers have a high interpersonal intelligence.

Exercise

● Use 'storytelling' to link ideas, facts and information. Just because it is maths or science does not mean it cannot be told as a story.

● Set out the information or facts in a clear order and then generate a story. Make it as fantastic and imaginative as possible, using all five senses.

133

- Do not write it down but talk through the story first either on your own or create it with one or two other people.

- When you have the story in your head tell it to someone else. Tell it to one other person or a group. Tell it to your parents or family members.

- When you have told the story several times and it is clear in your head write the story down and read it aloud.

- Use the Memory Matrix (see p.141) to review. When you review do this by either speaking it aloud or retelling it to someone else and get them to quiz you on the facts that you have included in the story to assist in recall and accuracy.

Further development

- When working at home, talk through the things you are about to study and revise and explain clearly to parents/family members what you are going to study and why.

- After you have completed your work go back and review what you have just done. Do this every time you study: explain, apply and review.

- Create a 'learning' group of friends and try to study together at least once a week. Be clear where and when you are meeting and make a commitment to them and yourself that you will get together to study and revise. Just having people around you will often be enough for you to feel more comfortable and focused.

- Discuss how you could make use of the information to further develop your learning, confidence and maturity.

- Once you recognize the importance of a supportive group, then you might want to timetable regular study time together.

- You may want to create different study groups for different subjects to further develop your support network.

2 Musical or rhythmic memory

Musical-rhythmic learners are sensitive to the sounds in their environment, including the inflections in the human voice. They enjoy music, and may listen to music when they study or read. They are skilled at recognizing pitch and rhythm. Learning through melody and music works well for people with high musical-rhythmic intelligence.

Exercise

- Work either on your own or with one or two of your friends (possibly those who are now acting as your learning support team).

- Find a popular song that you like and replace the lyrics to summarize the learning you are going to recall. You can write out the lyrics by hand or type them into a computer.

- Do this in pairs if musical learning is not your strength. However, the whole point of these memory exercises is for you to challenge all your learning styles, so do not just hand the task over to the more musical members of the group. They can take the lead but don't just sit back and expect someone else to do it – take ownership and be surprised by your own creativity!

Further development

- Once you have seen how speedy and effective this learning method is, find a subject or topic that you are studying and do the same thing. Re-write the lyrics to a song to summarize the learning.

- If you are very enterprising, do what a group of my past students did and work on a wide range of subjects to create lyrics, then burn the tunes onto a CD and sell them as study aids to the rest of the year group. (I believe they made nearly £400.)

3 Intrapersonal memory

Intrapersonal learners are aware of their own strengths, weaknesses and feelings. They are creative, independent and reflective thinkers. They usually possess self-confidence, determination and high motivation. They may respond with strong opinions when controversial topics are discussed. They learn best by engaging in independent study projects rather than working on group projects. Pacing their own instruction is important to them. Entrepreneurs, philosophers and psychologists all possess strong intrapersonal skills.

Exercise

- Get a blank notebook or diary.

- Go through your diary and book in at least 10 minutes a day (and I mean every day) for a week in order for you to have time on your own to think about what you have been doing and how you feel.

- Look at the Memory Matrix that you have used for earlier memory exercises. Review the information and reflect on how much effort you have or have not put into your own personal development as a learner.

135

● Keep the journal going for one week creating regular time to stop and think. Make notes on how you feel. You do not have to write much, but try to reflect on how you are feeling, and what action you are taking to further challenge your thinking and behaviour. Draw pictures if that is more useful to you.

Further development

● When you see the benefit of self-reflection, you may want to create daily and/or weekly time to review all your learning in this way – first on your own and then with your support group of friends, family and teachers.

4 Physical memory

Physical/practical or bodily-kinesthetic learners use physical sensations to gather information. They have good balance and co-ordination and are skilled with their hands. Learning tasks that provide physical activities and hands-on experiences work well for them. People with highly developed bodily-kinesthetic abilities include carpenters, mechanics, dancers, gymnasts, swimmers and jugglers.

Exercise

● Stand up and point to eight areas around the body:

head

eye

ear

nose

mouth

down your pants

feet

right hand

● You can have as many places around the body as you wish to store the information you need. I am going to use the eight places for remembering the eight kinds of intelligence.

● Link the intelligence to a person that you think has this as their main intelligence. I will list the intelligence and the name of the person that I am using as the link but come up with your own if you wish.

head – mathematical/analytical (Carol Vorderman)

eye – visual/spatial (Picasso)

ear – sound/music (Eminem)

nose – intrapersonal (Mahatma Gandhi)

mouth – verbal (William Shakespeare)

down your pants – naturalistic (Charlie Dimmock)

feet – physical (David Beckham)

right hand – interpersonal (Nelson Mandela)

- Go through the list in order and use the R.I.N.G. principle (relevant, interesting, naughty and a giggle) to create a strong mental image. For example: Carol Vorderman doing 'Countdown' on your head. Go through at least three of your five senses. Sound: 'Countdown' tune. Sight: what a lovely dress Carol has got on. Touch: can you feel Carol walking on your head? Smell: what perfume is Carol wearing, or does she need a bath? Taste: is Carol eating calculators and books? This is *your* imagination, so do not hold back.

- Wait for 20 minutes and then come back and review, going in order around the body, recalling the facts. Review again an hour later. **Use the Memory Matrix!**

Further development

Try this technique for remembering information, ideas and facts for other subjects.

- Combine the structure and physicality of learning with the Memory Matrix and you will soon speed up your brain.

- Remember: if you are physical and like sport then you should get physical and sporty with your learning as this will help your studies.

5 Logical-mathematical memory

Logical-mathematical intelligence is often linked with the term 'scientific thinking'. Logical-mathematical people like to explore patterns and relationships, to experiment, to ask questions and enjoy well-ordered tasks. They like to work with numbers and relish opportunities to solve problems via logical reasoning. They learn best by classifying information, using abstract thought, and looking for common basic principles and patterns. Many scientists have a high degree of logical-mathematical intelligence.

Exercise

- Get a fresh Memory Matrix sheet.

- Choose one subject that you find challenging or you need to focus on.

- On the back of the matrix, make a list of the key learning points. Seek clarity from the teacher on any points that you find vague or confusing. If you are shy, then speak to the teacher privately, sharing the matrix to highlight the fact that you are taking your learning seriously.

- Once you have grasped the key points, complete the matrix and **stick to the times!**

● Also, make sure that you have used visual (see it), auditory (hear it) and kinesthetic (do it) to reinforce the learning.

Further development

● Organize information sequentially or hierarchically. Both patterns can help you compare and contrast the material for similarities and differences.

● Copy key information from your notes and textbook into your computer. Use the printouts for visual review.

● Make flashcards of words and concepts that need to be memorized. Use highlighters to emphasize key points on the cards. Limit the amount of information per card so your mind can take a mental picture of the information.

● When learning information presented in diagrams or illustrations, write out explanations for the information.

● When learning mathematical or technical information, write out in key phrases how to do each step.

● Use large square graph paper to assist in creating charts and diagrams that illustrate key concepts.

● If you are experiencing difficulty in a class where most of the material is abstract and theoretical, do not get discouraged. Ask your teacher for specific examples of key concepts, or try to find some in your course text or other references.

6 Naturalistic memory

Naturalistic learners are in touch with nature and the outdoors, in terms of environment, animals, conservation, and so on. They sense patterns and are good at categorization. They are also keen planners and organizers of living areas. Naturalistic learners learn best studying natural phenomena in natural settings, understanding how things work. They may express interest in biology, zoology, botany, geography, geology, meteorology, paleontology or astronomy – fields directly connected to some aspect of nature.

Task

● Go outside and draw a simple garden design. If it is based on the shape of your own or a familiar garden this will support recall.

● Make sure there are eight key parts of the garden: for example, a patio, a water feature, a vegetable patch, a children's play area, a shed, a compost heap, an oak tree, a lawn.

● Whatever your design, make it colourful and imagine the joy of actually creating it. Allow yourself a few moments of daydreaming…

- Go round your garden and write the names of the eight intelligences. Include key words or short explanations of the main characteristics of each intelligence.

- Complete the Memory Matrix and review your 'learning garden' after 20 minutes.

- Review again after one hour.

Further development

- Create a 'learning garden design' for another subject and topic.

- Imagine the smells related to each area of the garden and see how your sense of smell can impact on your memory.

- When you revise, burn essential oils for different subjects or topics. When you have to take the exam or test put some drops of the particular oil that relates to the subject onto your wrist or a handkerchief, and sniff it during the test – it will spark up your brain and help your memory.

7 Visual-spatial memory

Visual-spatial people work well with maps, charts, diagrams and visual arts in general. They are able to visualize clear mental images. They like to design and create things. They learn best by looking at pictures and watching videos. Sculptors, painters, architects, surgeons and engineers are usually people with well-developed visual-spatial abilities.

Exercise

- Draw, design, photograph, or make a short animation or PowerPoint presentation to summarize the eight intelligences. Show what you have gained and how you have been able to move from 'knowing' to 'doing' by working on the exercises.

- Show the journey that you have been on, the challenges that you have had and how you have overcome them.

- Do this either on your own, in pairs or in a small team.

- Prepare a short presentation (not more than three minutes long) that you will present to your class or group.

Longer-term action

- Use visual images, designs and colour to record and recall your learning. I personally find mind mapping very effective. Do a search on the internet for 'mind mapping' and you'll find lots of very useful sites.

8 Verbal-linguistic memory

Verbal-linguistic learners have highly developed auditory skills, enjoy reading and writing, like to play word games, and have a good memory for names, dates and places. They like to tell stories, and get their point across. You learn best by saying and hearing words. Poets, writers, and people who speak a great deal in their jobs (like teachers) probably have a high degree of verbal-linguistic intelligence.

Exercise

- Prepare to give a focused and clear presentation of no more than three minutes, using the 'visual' aid you produced during the 'visual-spatial' task.

- You can work with others or on your own but make sure that you have rehearsed it and presented it at least three times before the day.

- Liaise with your teacher to make sure you have all that you need on the day in the way of technical support, space and equipment. If possible, try to do a technical rehearsal in the space where you will be doing the actual presentation.

- Make sure that your presentation is in three clear sections:

  introduction – who are you, what are you going to talk about, and so on.
  delivery – do your presentation
  summary – briefly summarize the main points and what the next steps could be.

- Speak clearly and not too fast.

Further development

- Show what you know – sit each day with your parents, or study group or family member, and talk through what you are going to study, and when you have done your study/homework talk through and share what you have done.

- A fun way for verbal people to learn is to record the key points and listen back to them. Better still, get someone you know and like to read the key points. Grandparents reading your study notes can be a very positive means of recall. Get them to read without their teeth in for a more advanced comedy element to further enhance learning (just think R.I.N.G.).

Memory Matrix

How to revise – based on the Ebbinghaus Curve of Forgetting

Reviewing or revising means 'looking through again'. If you don't go back and review, you will forget most of what you thought you'd learned. Reviewing shifts your learning from your short-term to your long-term memory by reinforcing the connections in your brain that help memory. We forget things if we don't allow ourselves the time to review. How can we make sure we find the time? This matrix may help you.

Try this! Choose a topic that you need to revise for a test. Show yourself that regular review works by making an effort to review the topic regularly and keeping a record of each time you review and how you work.

How to revise. Use your knowledge of yourself as a learner. Work to your strengths, using your preferred learning styles. If you do not know your strengths or areas for improvement I would recommend you go to www.networkcontinuum.co.uk and complete one.

Keeping the record. Note the time and date for each review; note the styles of learning you use. NB – some varieties of learning styles will keep the brain engaged and help to keep you motivated – try to use more than one across the review sequence.

Use it or lose it! Aim to complete a sequence of reviews to give yourself a fair chance to see whether this will work for you.

Topic	Review sequence	Date/time	Learning style			
			Visual e.g. mind-mapping; post-it notes	Auditory e.g. reading aloud; taping	Kinesthetic/tactile e.g. making; moving self or materials around	Other e.g. taste or smell
Key notes (Use the back of the sheet as well.)	1. Start					
	2. 20 minutes					
	3. 1 hour					
	4. 8 hours					
	5. 24 hours					
	6. 2 days					
	7. 5 days					
	8. 30 days					
	9. Review every few weeks till your exam or test.					

© Roy Leighton Associates Ltd 2006

141

A life by the sea

Trisha Lee

"Look after your little sister," Mum shouted up the stairs that morning.

"Why?" snapped Vanessa.

"I'm working this afternoon," Mum replied, "and anyway that's what good big sisters do!"

"I'm not a good big sister, she gets on my nerves, and I don't want to look after her," Vanessa muttered angrily under her breath.

Bang! – the front door shut, and all chance of winning the argument ceased.

"Nessy, Nessy, play with me," five-year-old Amanda pleaded but Vanessa wasn't listening.

As far as she was concerned her little sister was too demanding. "Nessy do this, Nessy do that." Nessy wanted to go out on her own, with her own mates, she wanted to have fun – "But oh no, it's the school holidays and Mum can't get a babysitter so I'm shut up at home playing good big sister."

"I wish she never existed, I wish I lived in a fortress where no little sisters were allowed and outside was all dark so that no one could come near," whispered Vanessa vindictively.

This was a shame, because in the room across the corridor Amanda was also thinking about sisters. "My big sister is the best sister in the world. I love it when Mum goes out to work and it's just me and Nessy. I wish our house was an island surrounded by water and it was just me and Nessy, and nobody and no boats could come near."

Beware of what you wish for, for when the Moon is still visible in the sky at midday, and the day you're in the middle of is Thursday, who knows what might come true?

And down the street began to flow a trickle of water. At first it was just a drop, a little spill, a tiny unnoticeable splash, but as each drop mingled with every spill and joined together with every splash a torrent of water began to form.

Unknown to the girls inside, waves began to circle around their house, crashing against their garden and breaking the join between their little home and the neighbourhood that enclosed them. As more and more water poured by, the house began to move, to float; to tear away from the others, heading downstream, out into the ocean, far, far away.

"Nessy, I'm bored!" Amanda called once again at the door to her sister's room. "Tell me a story, read to me, play with me." But the door remained closed. "Nessy, I know you're in there, are you playing hide and seek, 'cos if you are, I've found you, let me in."

"Leave me alone," Vanessa called through the bedroom door. "I don't want to play with you, I'm busy. Why don't you go outside in the garden and play, have some fresh air, I'll do you some dinner in half an hour."

So Amanda went downstairs, put on her outdoor shoes and opened the door.

"Wow, Nessy, we live by the sea!" shouted Amanda. "Nessy, it's amazing, number 5's gone, and number 7's gone. Nessy, all the houses have gone, please come and see. I'm going to get my fishing net and see if I can catch a great big fish for tea. And I'm going to get my binoculars and see if I can see any boats."

Amanda rushed around the house gathering suitable things for a life by the sea. She picked up her favourite towel, for drying her toes after splashing around in the water; she found a jam jar to put any fish in that she might catch. She tied a piece of string around the top of it to make it easier to carry. Then she picked up her mother's suntan cream just in case the sea air gave her sunburn. Ready and prepared for her big day out she once again stood at the door, opened it, and smiled happily to herself at the sight of all that water.

"Nessy, I'm ready now. Come and have a look at the sea, it's all around us. Please come and play in the sea with me," Mandy called out once more to her sister.

But all was quiet from behind Vanessa's bedroom door.

"Well, I'm going out on my own then, I won't go further than the garden. Well, I can't really because it's all water. But please come and play with me, it's really sunny out here," pleaded Amanda.

Realizing that, as usual, Vanessa wasn't going to answer, Mandy ran out into the sunlight clutching in her small hands all her treasures for a new life by the sea and gently closing the door behind her.

144

Vanessa was sitting on her bed, looking through her CD collection and playing odd songs to herself as the mood struck her. She heard Mandy prattling on about living by the sea and how it was surrounding them, but that didn't surprise her. Mandy was always inventing something. Active imagination, her Mum called it. Not telling the truth was Nessy's opinion – still, if it kept her quiet…

She was aware that Mandy was running up and down the stairs collecting things from different rooms, but music was blaring out of her Walkman at the time so she didn't give it too much attention. And she also heard Amanda plead with her to come and play outside in the sun.

But Nessy had no intention of budging. Well, she had no intention of budging, until the front door closed and all sorts of strange things began to occur.

First there was a short loud sound, like two metallic objects scraping against each other, and then the slam of something closing noisily and violently. Crash, bang, clang. High-pitched ringing sounds, accompanied by harsh, tinny, rattling and scraping noises, scratching and scraping, scratching and scraping, echoing round the house.

This time Nessy did get off the bed.

She shot out of her room, ran down the top corridor, and then froze. The house around her was slowly changing. Where once there had been subtle pink wallpaper with tiny rosebuds and matching borders, the walls were now becoming covered in dark wooden mahogany, and swords and shields and various other forms of armour were beginning to appear, hanging on the wall, as if by magic.

The stair carpet was slowly disappearing, and being replaced by a harsh cold stone floor. And all these transformations were accompanied by the most awful din imaginable, as wood creaked open to be replaced by stone, and walls moved further and further apart to make larger rooms and Vanessa's house turned itself slowly into a lonely fortress.

"Mandy, Mandy, where are you?" Surprisingly, Nessy's first thoughts were for her sister's safety.

She rushed to the front door, remembering Mandy had wandered outside not two minutes earlier. The door was unrecognizable. It had grown beyond the proportions of the small house, and now stood, ten feet high, thick, solid wood – covered on every inch of its right-hand side in bolts, locks and chains.

Vanessa grabbed at the first bolt and undid it quickly, and then as fast as she could she began to work down the side of the door, turning keys and drawing bolts, opening padlocks and loosening chains. But every time she got about halfway down, the bolts and locks and keys and padlocks she had already opened were magically relocking, closing before her very eyes.

145

"Mandy, Mandy! Are you alright?" she called out to the world behind the locked door. She ran to the window and peered out, hoping to catch a glimpse of her sister but everything outside was in darkness. The sun looked as if it had long ago set on this world and nothing could penetrate the blackness.

"Mandy, Mandy!" she called at the top of her voice. "Are you still out there? Come to the window and let me see your face."

Her words were greeted with silence.

Meanwhile, Mandy sat in the garden, fishing. Her small net dangled into the water as she peered in deep concentration into the ocean that surrounded her and tried to catch something bigger than the strange little black dots and quickly moving see-through things she had so far managed to tip into her jam jar. Nessy still hadn't come out but Mandy was happy enough, playing in her own sea world, not worrying about her sister. She was beginning to feel a bit peckish though. Nessy had said she'd make dinner soon. Mandy headed back towards the house.

The front door slid open, the bolts disappearing as if they had never existed. Nessy ran towards it, towards the garden where her sister must be, but when she reached the door all she could see was cold, all-encompassing darkness, swallowing up the world. She stood nervously on the doorstep, too frightened to go out and look for her sister, and too scared to shut the door and give up hope of ever seeing her again.

"Mandy!" she called out in sheer panic.

"Nessy?" came the gentle reply. "Is dinner nearly ready? I'm starving."

"Where are you?" Vanessa called out, looking wildly up and down the dark patch of air in front of her.

"Are we playing hide and seek?" Mandy replied. "Can't you see me? You're pretty warm. I'm in the garden."

"I can't see anything," said Nessy, "it's too dark"

Mandy began to laugh. She wasn't sure what game her big sister was playing but it sounded really funny. Nessy was standing at the door, waving her arms in front of her and looking around all over the place, pretending she couldn't see her younger sister. Mandy fell to the ground in hysterics.

"Why are you laughing?" shouted Nessy.

"Because it's such a funny game," replied Mandy, "and you never normally play with me, and you look so funny moving your head around so much and peering at me. Come and see the sea, come fishing with me. I love living on this island."

"But I can't see the sea, I can't see anything," Nessy replied. "I can't even see you."

"That's all right," said Mandy. "I'll hold your hand, then you'll be able to see the sea with me."

Mandy held out her hand, watching quizzically as her sister groped the air around her until slowly she found it and their fingers entwined. Hands safely joined, Mandy began to walk back towards the edge of the garden and the beautiful blue sea that surrounded her house. She had only taken a few steps before she felt her sister shudder and freeze.

"Is it safe?" Nessy asked. "I can't see a thing and I feel like I'm going to fall down an enormous hole with every step. I don't know how you can see anything in this darkness, but it's sure as hell scaring me. I'd go back to the house if I could see which direction it was in."

Mandy looked at her sister. The sun was shining brightly above them and she could see sea gulls flying around at the edge of her garden, but if this was the game Nessy wanted to play then Mandy was so happy to be included that she was prepared to go along with it whatever happened.

"Pretend you're the princess and I'm your unicorn, and you've been left in the dark by a wicked witch and I have galloped over to save you. And when you touch the silvery mane of my hair it starts to glow, brighter and brighter around you. And as you hold on to me my mane throws out the most magical light you have ever seen and if you walk close to me you can see your way easily, each step is lit up and you begin to feel safe."

And as Nessy walked in the darkness outside her house, holding onto her young sister's hand she felt suddenly safe. Reaching up, she touched her sister's long blonde hair and as it fell through her fingers she imagined the call of the unicorn and the bright light spilling in front of her. Slowly, bit by bit, she could just make out her way, a tiny bit of ground, a stone, a bit of the path, one of the daffodils that had just opened its yellow head. If she looked up too quickly the darkness engulfed her again, but if she trusted her sister, the magical unicorn, then the ground in front of her was light enough to see.

Mandy led her sister down to the end of the garden. The waves lapped at the gate and the gulls flew around in the air and cried out their happy song to the sun. But Nessy, trapped in the darkness outside her fortress, could hear nothing. To her the world was silent and dark.

"Can you see the sea?" called Mandy as she watched her sister flinch. Nessy, eyes wide open, looking this way and that, shook her head.

"I can see nothing but blackness. I can hear nothing but your voice and the silence of the air in the dead of night. Hold my hand, for it makes me feel braver, and tell me what the sea is like."

Amanda began to describe the sea to her older sister. She told Nessy how the sun shone on the water and caught the waves in little ripples forming patches of pure gold. She talked of the sea's lullaby, and how the wind on the water rubbed together so much that the waves sung to the world, sssssh, sssssh, sssssh. And she described the whole picture, a little three-bedroom house, with a chimney and a red door, in the middle of a green, green lawn, with borders of flowers of every colour and a white wooden fence, surrounded by ocean.

Mandy told her sister how two girls sat in the garden, one, the younger, with silver blonde hair, holding the hand of her dark-haired older sister and telling her stories to help her see.

Nessy sat next to her, listening carefully, closing her eyes so that she could see the ocean.

As the day wore on, the two girls stayed together in the garden. They lay down and Nessy placed her arm around her little sister, and, finally, hearing the waves lapping against the white garden fence, she could see it all for the first time. And Nessy opened herself up to a life by the sea.

Listening intently

Trisha Lee

A nine year old boy sits in the Foundation Stage classroom of a Lewisham primary school. He listens intently to the story dictated to him by a four year old child. His pen is poised above the page; his concentration is engraved on his face as he prepares to write:

> Spiderman grab the ice-cream man and got all the ice-cream, but all the ice-cream men eat all the ice-cream and Spiderman break the ice-cream man car and make a fire. Ice-cream man gets in a car and crashed up another car to fire. Spiderman shout at the car and Spiderman climbed up the ice-cream man and then he fell.

The nine year old interrupts the story at various points, needing to repeat the words out loud so he can write them down verbatim. The four year old is familiar with this technique and patiently waits for the older child to finish each sentence before proceeding. Other young children crowd around, listening to this story, eagerly awaiting their turn. Maybe their stories will borrow some of the images of this narrative and today the classroom will echo with 'ice-cream man' adventures.

A girl steps forward. She has been waiting patiently for her turn and smiles as she takes her seat by another nine year old:

> Once upon a time there was a beautiful princess and she had lots of friends. And when she went home her friends were gone and she was crying. She called her mummy and she said 'mummy, all my friends are gone'. And her friends all called their mummy and daddy 'all my friends are gone'. And they were all crying, and when they stopped crying they found each other. And they went to the park.

The older girl who scribes this story shows empathy with the plight of the younger child. She too knows the sadness of having no friends. 'I'm glad she found them all again,' she murmurs at the end of the story and the two children look at each other for a moment, sharing a secret vulnerability that the younger child was able to articulate far more easily than her older counterpart. The two girls walk hand in hand to the carpet where the rest of the class are gathering.

Having completed their storytelling, the Reception children seat themselves expectantly around a taped-out stage. This is where they will act out their stories. The Year 5 pupils who have been scribing for them all afternoon settle on chairs and begin reading each story aloud, signalling to children around the stage to leave their places and take on the roles ascribed. At first, they read quietly, with some uncertainty. At each character they stop and ask the child whose turn it is to get up on the stage to show 'how Spiderman moves' or 'how the ice-cream man eats all the ice-cream'. As time progresses these young leaders become more confident, using their hands to beckon shyer children onto the stage and praising their younger peers. The Reception children are equally patient, seeming to understand how hard it must be for the older child and responding well to voices that are quieter than the ones they are used to. The technique is not as speedy as when the adults run it, but this is early days and confidence is growing in both age groups.

What is most apparent, and most exciting, is the value that these children place on each other, regardless of age. All the children in this classroom listen intently to each other. According to Judith Harris, in *The Nurture Assumption* (1999), our peers are those who above all others have the strongest influence on us; they have the power to shape what we wear, effect how we feel about ourselves and even impact on our adult personalities. Harris rates influence from the peer group more highly than influence from parents or any other kind of adult social group. If this is so, then schools have in each classroom valuable resources that they can tap into in the form of peer group learning and motivation.

On a purely social/emotional level I have seen evidence that it works. Place a difficult older child with a younger child in need of support and there can be surprising results. I once knew a 12-year-old boy who was constantly in trouble, at school, at home, on the streets. He was always in fights, always cussing someone or something, always getting angry and running off in a strop. He was hard work. But one day I saw a new side to him. He had come to the youth theatre – although he was always angry about something he was one of our most regular attenders – but this week he had brought with him his seven year old cousin.

'He's staying round my house. Me mam said I have to bring him or I can't come.' I agreed – it was better to bring the cousin than to miss a rehearsal. But that night I saw a different side to that 12-year-old boy: for that night he became the most caring, attentive, supportive and friendly child I had ever seen. He wanted to make sure his younger cousin felt relaxed and he went out of his way to ensure that he made this happen. As the weeks went on I began to observe him with younger children. He was never the bully, always the great friend and supporter, and the way he listened intently would have taught many adults a thing or two.

When older pupils work with younger children it enhances their confidence. I have seen pupils who are shy or reluctant to join in within their own classroom gain in self-belief as a result of being away from their own age group. If these feelings are nurtured and allowed to grow, then this confidence will carry over into all areas of their life.

For children who are struggling with attainment at their current level another enormous benefit is gained when they cover an area of learning which they now find easy. Passing on to someone younger a skill about which they now feel secure helps them to cement their own learning. In order to teach you have to understand. For example, during the peer group education project one Year 5 boy who had problems with writing suddenly gained two attainment points in only four weeks. His SENCO believed that he suddenly found a purpose for his writing and being able to concentrate on only that aspect of literacy rather than on writing and composing sentences at the same time had freed him up.

Getting older pupils to work as scribes is one possible way of utilizing peer group education in the classroom, but there are many other ways in which older children can support and lead the work of their younger peers.

At Dartington Primary School in Totnes, Devon, the staff developed a Primary Qualified Teacher Status (PQTS) course where pupils from Year 5 were introduced to basic teaching skills. The pupils involved in the programme crafted lesson plans, observed teachers at work, and selected the reward systems they put into place with a Year 1 class in order to deliver a lesson on English or maths at the end of the term. A documentary about the work is available on the Teachers TV website (www.teachers.tv) and includes feedback from both pupils and staff.

Other approaches include visits by older pupils to younger classrooms with the aim of reading stories. Adapting this idea slightly, MakeBelieve Arts recently piloted a programme entitled 'Year 6 as Storytellers' where pupils spent time rehearsing stories in small groups which they then performed to Foundation Stage pupils.

A surprising benefit arose from this work; older pupils became less restricted in their acting as a result of performing to a younger age group. This freeing up has become apparent in other projects. One very restricted class of Year 5 pupils suddenly became imaginative storytellers purely because I split the class and mixed each group up with half of a Year 3 class and asked them to write stories and act them out for the benefit of the younger pupils. Although the Year 5 believed that they were helping the Year 3s, to me the learning was happening the other way round. I witnessed Year 3 pupils reminding Year 5 how to be creative and to play effectively.

Another benefit is the positive reception given by younger children to their older peers. This uncritical approach is one of the most rewarding aspects of peer group education. In storytelling and story acting, older pupils do not need to worry about their writing or spelling ability as the younger children will not judge them.

A girl who previously had whispered her stories to an adult (so inaudibly that to hear her meant placing your ear as close to her mouth as possible) was witnessed speaking loudly and clearly as she dictated her now much longer story to the Year 5 pupil. This happened within days of Year 5 entering the classroom. Maybe it was because she knew that the older girl who was taking her story had not yet developed the skill of listening as intently as her normally quiet voice demanded. Maybe it meant more to her that the older child understood her words. For whatever reason, however, her confidence and the clarity of her voice changed beyond recognition as the two age groups worked together to get her story down.

The patience shown by older children when entering the Nursery and Reception classroom always astonishes me. One day a four year old sat drinking his milk at the story table. He had sat down to dictate his story but his milk had proved more interesting and he sucked on the straw in silence for five minutes. The older child next to him waited patiently, only once interrupting his drink to ask if he was ready to tell his story. When the four year old carried on drinking, the older boy waited, looked around, fiddled with some of his crayons, but showed no form of impatience. Eventually the drink was finished and the story began. I was impressed. It made me realize how often as adults we try to rush children: 'Do it now, you can do that later.' Here was a four year old who needed the time, couldn't be rushed but ended up telling a story that might never have been born if he hadn't been allowed to gather his thoughts over a carton of milk.

A Reception class teacher wondered if the praise a Year 5 pupil gives a younger child is somehow different, more powerful. Perhaps children learn to expect praise from their teacher but it has more weight behind it when it comes from older children. She could see her class visibly grow in stature when an older pupil commented that something they had done was excellent.

For Year 5 pupils the observations have been even more revealing. It became apparent that during storytelling and story acting many children are really keen to write down accurately and precisely what their younger peers are saying. It was noted that they took more time and care over their spellings, handwriting and letter formation than they usually did, even though they were told that in this instance none of this was important as long as they could read what they had written. It was as if the older children realized the importance of this writing, believing that here it served a real purpose and that they were responsible in their role as scribes to get it right for the younger child.

The usefulness of this way of working is that, instead of having to think and write at the same time, scribes simply have to write, and storytellers simply have to think. This reduces stress for many children, and frees them up for the task in hand.

When a four year old tells a story that ends with the words 'and then history was happy again' and a nine year old boy who lacks confidence in his own writing is able to comment before his peers on the 'beauty of this ending' then surely here is a way of working that benefits the richness of language in both age groups and creates a community of mixed aged learning that truly values the stories and abilities of each other.

Peer group education

Older children in younger classrooms: a practical approach

Trisha Lee

In the same way that adults need preparation time before entering the school classroom, it is important that young people as peer group educators are given time to prepare and train in the programme of work that they are about to deliver. Time spent at the beginning of this process will mean that children have much more confidence when they finally enter the lower age group classrooms.

I will divide the process into two areas: firstly, children who are entering the Foundation Stage classroom to tell stories to younger children and secondly, to scribe stories from younger children.

Children as storytellers in younger classrooms

Logistics

The preferred age group for this activity is Year 5 or above. It is better if children rehearse the stories in small groups. The optimum size for each group is five pupils. Children should be given time to work individually as well, in time set aside by the teacher to help shape and polish each story. The stories can be read, with each child in the group sharing the narration, or preferably narrated and brought to life via enactment and drama.

Preparation

Select six children's stories suitable for Nursery, Reception and Year 1 pupils. This will ensure that you have a different story for each group to work on. The choice of stories could be made in collaboration with Foundation Stage teachers. Arrange with Foundation Stage and Year 1 classes to become the audience for your pupils' work once the stories are ready.

Rehearsals

Before introducing storytelling it is helpful to warm up with some storytelling exercises.

A story in five parts

Tell the children that they are going to tell a story in just five parts:

1 Introduction

2 Development

3 Conflict

4 Climax

5 Conclusion.

Start with a well-known story, for example 'Red Riding Hood'. Ask the children to give you an action and a sound (or short phrase) to serve as the introduction to the story. Let the children talk about this for a while. What is the most important thing that happens at the beginning of the story, remembering that we have only five parts?

If the consensus of opinion is that the Introduction is Red Riding Hood's mother packing a bag for her to take to grandma's, then ask for an action and a sound that sums this up. The action might be people filling an imaginary basket and the sound could be a hum or even a more sinister sound accompanied by the wag of a finger as the mother warns Red Riding Hood not to talk to strangers.

Once the action and sound are agreed, tell the class that whenever you say the word 'Introduction' they have to repeat that action and sound. Practise a couple of times. Next, move on to the word 'Development': what happens next in the story to develop the plot? Perhaps it is the wolf watching Red Riding Hood from behind a tree. Get the class to agree on an action and sound that accompanies this. Practise moving from 'Introduction' and its action and sound to 'Development' and the new action and sound. In this way, work through 'Conflict', 'Climax' and 'Conclusion', stopping at each point to agree on an action and sound for each part of the story, and practising moving from one to the other as each of the words are called out.

When you have reached the Conclusion and agreed on all the actions and sounds it is time to tell the story of Little Red Riding Hood in five parts. Introduce this to an imaginary

155

audience and get the class to move through the actions and sounds for one last time, as you call out the order.

After the children have become familiar with this technique you can get them to use it for a whole range of stories, and even as a way of creating their own stories in five parts.

Actors/narrators

Once again, begin this process by working with a well-known story. Fairy stories are brilliant for this as they have universal appeal and most children know them even if it takes a few reminders to jog their memory of the exact order of events.

Ask the class for four volunteers who know the story of, for example, 'Goldilocks and the Three Bears'. Tell the children that before they volunteer they need to be sure they know the story well enough to tell it to the rest of the group.

Once the four children are ready, get them to stand at the front of the room and ask the first child to begin telling the story. Inform them beforehand that at various points you will say the word 'Pass', and the story then has to move to the next person along in the line.

Let the rest of the class know that they are to be the actors and that you want them to get up and act out in mime not only the people but the objects and the scenery that go towards creating this story.

Tell the storytellers to watch what the actors are doing as they can control the shape of the action with their own words.

Once the story starts, get the actors to come up and enact the various parts. Bring up children to play the three bears, the cottage and the bowls of porridge. Remember to keep saying 'Pass' so that the story gets passed from one narrator to another ensuring that all four children get an equal share.

This technique can at times seem a little chaotic but it works really well with children from as young as Year 4 through to adults. It is a great way of incorporating children's play and imagination alongside the skill of developing storytelling techniques.

Bringing the story to life

Once the children are in groups give each group a copy of the story you have chosen for them to work on. It is important that these stories are short and easy to read.

Set each group the task of reading their story and then finding a way of telling it in five parts. Once they have practised these, they can be shared with the class.

Next, work with the children on how they will tell their story. Do they want to enact various parts alongside the narration or do they just wish to share the narration between each other?

If children have problems keeping their story acting in a confined area, tape out a small square stage on the floor and tell them that all their acting must take place in this area. Spend time helping children to adopt a storytelling voice: talk about volume and quietness, creepy voices and sad voices, and how important the voice is in pulling the audience in.

Once the groups are confident with their stories arrange for them to visit the lower school and perform to the younger children.

Further development

Pupils who thrive on book stories can be pushed further next time. Ask them to work on the retelling of a well-known story which is not written down. Finally, if your class really take to this work then involve them in creating their own stories for younger pupils and work on ways to bring these stories to life.

Story map: a way into creating children's own stories

Draw a wavy diagonal line from the top of large piece of paper on the left-hand side to the bottom of the paper on the right-hand side.

Point to the top of the line and ask the class to agree on an object or a person or a place that can go there. Once there is agreement draw whatever has been suggested and then move to the middle of the line and repeat the same question. Again draw whatever object or place or person is suggested. Next ask the same for the end of the line, the section between the middle and the beginning of the line, and the section between the middle and the end of the line. Once this is done your wavy line should have five drawings on it.

Ask children to suggest the narrative that connects these pictures together. The first picture is the introduction to the story, the second is the development, and so on. See what stories are created in this way and how instinctively our brains seek to make connections between objects.

157

You could also develop this idea by giving every member of the class a piece of paper with a wavy line going vertically down the page. Ask the children to draw at the top of the line an object, place or person. Then get them to fold down their picture to hide it and pass their paper on to the person next to them. This person draws another object, place or person and again folds the paper so that their picture cannot be seen. Keep going until each line has five pictures on it. The paper then gets handed on one more time and it is the sixth person who unfolds it and has to try and create a narrative connection between the images.

Children as story scribes in younger classrooms

Logistics

- The preferred age group for this activity is Year 5 or above. If it can be arranged across primary and secondary schools it would be a great citizenship and literacy activity for Year 8 pupils to get involved in, returning to primary one morning a week to work within Foundation Stage classrooms.

- Although it is possible to pass on the technique to the whole class it is better to send only three or four children at a time into the younger age group classroom.

- For the technique to work fully there needs to be a strong partnership and understanding between the teachers in the lower age and the older age classroom.

- It is preferable that older pupils visit classes where the teacher is already using the Helicopter Technique of storytelling and story acting (see pages 41–52) so that the older pupils are not solely responsible for passing on the technique.

Master class – developing skills as scribes
Preparation

- Have a copy of the introductory story and a selection of other stories available (Figs 1 and 2, see end of this chapter).

- Photocopy examples of stories for the class to examine (Fig. 2).

- Photocopy the rules for scribing (Fig. 3).

- Photocopy the A and B slips (Fig. 4).

- Make sure you have plenty of masking tape.

The following bullet points suggest ways to approach handing on the technique of storytelling and story-acting to a class of Year 5 or 6 pupils. Depending on the group, these activities will take varying amounts of time; or you may decide to spend longer on one aspect of the work than another. Do not feel rushed in the delivery of these sessions: the more preparation you can do with a class the easier it will be for them when they enter the Foundation Stage classroom.

- Introduce the Helicopter Technique of storytelling and story acting to the group as described on pages 41–52. Tape out a rectangular stage on the floor and using the introductory stories supplied (Figs 1 and 2) involve the class in acting out these stories.

- After everyone has had a go at acting out collect two or three stories from the older children, find out which character they wish to be and immediately involve the class in acting out these stories.

- Ask the children what they notice about the way you have introduced the technique to them. Maybe they notice the way you move around the circle to cast children for their role on the stage; perhaps they notice the praise that you continue to give throughout their work; maybe it's how you ask them to show you the actions that they are doing. Make a note on a large sheet of paper of whatever they notice about how the work evolved.

- Hold your hand up as if you are holding an imaginary bowl and then begin stirring with an imaginary spoon. As soon as you have begun to do this, ask the class to pretend you are cooking. At least 95 per cent will end up copying your actions. Keep stirring and ask them what has happened? When they notice that they are all doing the same ask them why. Next, put your hands on your lap and ask them again to pretend they are cooking, but this time you don't do anything. Discuss with the class the difference in their responses. Relate this to how young children learn and how we can end up leading too much without meaning too.

- Hand out some examples of stories (Fig. 2) that 3–5-year-old children have told in the past and find out what the older children think of them. What do they like, what don't they like?

- Introduce rules for scribing (Fig. 3) and talk about the following:

  How you sit when taking stories so that the younger children can see what is written on the page.
  Each story should be only one page long (A5).
  Making eye contact with the younger child.
  Repeating back what is said word for word as you write it down.
  Encouraging and praising the younger child at all times.

- Practise getting the class scribing stories by telling them a story in short sentences which they have to scribe and say the words aloud as they write them. If you say 'Once upon a time there was a dog', then the whole class needs to scribe together and say 'Once upon a time there was a dog'. Make sure they also get used to writing the storyteller's name in the top right-hand corner of the page.

● Divide the class into pairs and tell them to decide who will be A and who will be B. Hand out the scribing story slips for A and B (Fig. 4). These need to be kept secret so that neither party is aware of what is written on his partner's slip. The children will also each need a sheet of A5 paper and a pencil. Next, ask the children to take it in turns telling a story to their partner. Their partner must write down the story word for word, but must also follow the mood suggested on their slip.

● Talk about how each partner felt when they told their story to the other person. Did anything annoy them? What felt like the most positive way of telling their story? What sort of response did they want?

● Take time getting children to lead the class in the acting out of their stories. If you have run this as a whole-class activity it may take time to get them all acted out, so you may need to spread this over a longer period of time. If the stories were taken on a Monday, then over the next five days (for 15 minutes a day) the class could act all of the remaining stories. In 15 minutes you should be able to act out between five and seven stories.

Once the children have practised scribing stories from each other it is a good time to send small groups of them down to the Foundation Stage classroom to try out what they have learned. Ask them to keep a diary of their thoughts and feelings, and take time to find out how it went with the infant teacher.

Master class – developing skills in leading acting out

Preparation

● Photocopy points for acting out sheet (Fig. 5).

● Photocopy and cut up the 'encouraging younger children onto the stage' slips (Fig. 6).

● Photocopy and cut up specific action requests (Fig. 7).

Once the children are confident in scribing stories it is worth spending time with them to work through some of the logistics of leading the acting out of stories. This is often the hardest part of the process for adults as well as children.

● First, ask the class to list all the words of praise they can think of (brilliant, fantastic, well done, and so on.) Write these up on a large sheet of paper. Next, get the class to discuss how they feel when they are encouraged or praised? Why do they think it is important to encourage Nursery or Reception-aged children?

● Ask the whole group to recite some of the praise words together in the most earnest and meaningful way possible. Then work round the class so that all the children practise praising each other: 'Nadia, that was lovely'; 'Safer, that was great'; and so on. Make sure that everyone tries hard to be sincere in their praise.

● Hand out the points for acting out sheets (Fig. 5) and get the class to read through and discuss them.

Encouraging younger children onto the stage...

Hand out photocopies of the 'encouraging younger children onto the stage' slips (Fig. 6). Talk to the class about the importance of getting children up onto the stage as quickly as possible, and about using encouraging voices and words. Get different children to read out the slips at the front of the class, and encourage them to be as persuasive as possible in inviting others to come and join them. Make sure that the person who is reading the slip makes eye contact and points and uses their hand to encourage someone up onto the stage.

Asking to see an action

Invite a group of about three children onto the taped-out stage. Tell them that they can do an action only when they are asked specifically to do it. Then hand the other children slips of paper with specific action requests (Fig. 7) and practise asking for these and watching the results. Remind the children asking for the actions to praise the three in the middle once they have finished acting. Keep changing the children's roles so that everyone has a turn at asking to see an action, praising or getting to act out.

161

Putting all this together

Get the group back into pairs to scribe another story from their partners. This time they should all be acting enthusiastically and encouragingly. Then begin to act out some of the stories but this time add all the additional layers that have just been practised.

Encourage the children to reflect on how well they and each of their peers are doing and allow the pupils to spend time in the younger classrooms practising and improving their skills as well as scribing and leading the acting out of stories within their own age group.

Evaluation

Once all the pupils involved in the project have had a chance to try out the technique with younger children begin a discussion about how it went and what they learned from the experience. Here are some points you might like them to consider:

- How did they feel it went?

- What did they find easy?

- What did they find hard?

- Was it how they expected?

Thoughts from Year 5 pupils who have worked in this way

- 'I found it hard to understand the children 'cos some of them they spoke different and they couldn't pronounce the words properly.'

- 'I was expecting the stories to be one word or a thought and when I went there they were long and good. And they were interesting.'

- 'The hardest thing was to write the story fast, the children said it quickly and then nearly half way finished the story, so I didn't get time to write all of it. I just had to be quick.'

- 'You can learn from the little children. People might think that children can't tell good stories, but when they get the experience that children can tell good stories they'll think, "oh so I was wrong then".'

- 'The stories are really imaginative although the younger children don't know what figurative means they are figurative stories.'

Note

Some sections of this chapter appeared previously in 'Listen! Do you want to hear a story? So let me begin', *EYE* (Early Years Education), 6, 10, Feb 2005, pp 12–14.

Figure 1

Introduction story

For another introduction story, see practical technique in pages 41–52.

One day three skipping turtles…

Let's see these three children playing skipping turtles, one, two, three. How do you think turtles skip?

And the butterfly says, 'Turtles don't skip.'

Let's see, can you be the butterfly, and can I hear you saying, 'Turtles don't skip'?

Then a deer says, 'If you skip you can't be a turtle.'

You play the deer – can you show me how the deer moves, and let's hear you say the words.

But they keep skipping and they keep on skipping, because some turtles can skip.

Figure 2

Examples of stories told by 4–5 year olds

A girl was walking through a jungle and a crocodile came and she ran, and she ran home because she was scared of the crocodile and the crocodile was eating her because she didn't like him. Then she ran so fast because she liked to, and she ran out of breath.

Once upon a time a girl and her mum and the monster, and the mum and girl said 'can we have some money'. The monster said 'no'. And they got poorly and dead.

There was a girl walking, she saw a big monster. Then she run as fast as she can and a dinosaur just got her and eat her. She learnt how to get out. She was growing up.

A caterpillar went to see his mummy. Then a big giant came and it squashed the hole. The caterpillar's hole. Gone…

Once I saw a princess, afterwards she just vanished and I searched for her everywhere. But I found her laying under her seat in bed and I carefully taked her out and put her to sleep on her bed and she was so beautiful.

A butterfly and the monster ate the butterfly. And the monster falled in the crocodile water and there was two crocodiles. And there was lots of crocodiles eating the butterfly, and then the butterfly was still alive. And there was a giant. And the giant scared of the monster. Then the butterfly killed the monster and the boy played in the sand.

Figure 3

Rules for scribing

1   Leave a space between each line.

2   Use large writing and write as fast as you can.

3   Repeat the whole sentence the child has dictated.

4   Then write this word for word.

5   Say each word as you write it down.

6   When finished, read it back to the child, underlining the characters as you read.

7   Ask the child which character they would like to play, and read them the list of characters you have underlined.

Suggested phrases

1   So, tell me your story.

2   Is there any more to your story?

Important points for acting out

1   Read story to first character or action.

2   Get people up with great speed, from their place in the circle.

3   Ask to see the action or movement.

4   Praise.

5   Read to next character or action and repeat above.

6   At end of story involve the group in clapping thank you.

7   Clear the stage.

Figure 4

Scribing story slips

Person A   When you take the story from your partner, act as if you are really interested and encourage them often. You can add in any of the following sentences if you think they need more encouragement.

> Wow, that is excellent.
> That's really good.
> Oh, I like that idea.
> Well done.

Person B   When you take the story from your partner behave as if you are bored and impatient and keep saying some of the following sentences.

> Hurry up.
> Are you finished yet?
> Is that all?
> That's not very good.

Person A   When you take the story from your partner, act as if you are really interested and encourage them often. You can add in any of the following sentences if you think they need more encouragement.

> Wow, that is excellent.
> That's really good.
> Oh, I like that idea.
> Well done.

Person B   When you take the story from your partner behave as if you are bored and impatient and keep saying some of the following sentences.

> Hurry up,
> Are you finished yet?
> Is that all?
> That's not very good

Figure 5

Points for acting out stories

1   Read story up to the first character or action point.

2   Get people up from their place around the circle.

3   Ask to see the action or phrase.

4   Praise.

5   Read to next character and repeat steps 1–4.

6   At end of story involve group in clapping thank you.

7   Clear the stage.

Figure 6

Encouraging younger children onto the stage

Come on then, you be the mummy, up you get…

And you? Come and be the puppy. No, ok
(move to person next to the one refusing), you be the puppy.

I need three bears, 1, 2, 3. Up you come.

A dog, come on, up you get, you be the dog…

And a dragon, you be the dragon, come on…

You be the ship, up you get…

Figure 7

Specific action requests

Can you show me how you make a rainbow?

Show me how the frog moves?

How does the tiger move? Is there a sound?

Can you show me a little teapot?

How might you be a house? Show me?

How does the elephant move?

Can you two show me how you'd make a well? And now can I see the fairy fall down the well?

Can I see the children sleeping?

How would you show the tooth turn into a coin?

Can you pretend to be the girl climbing onto the lion? Can I see her fall off?

Can I see the mummy in the car?

Can you show me how the dragon moves?

Can I see you pretending to throw the monster in the fire?

What goes around comes around

Tim Harding

Frank liked the sound of the clock. The clock that had always sat on the shelf above the fireplace of his home for as long as he could remember – and that must have been sixty years or more! Not a grand clock – or even a grandfather clock. Just a small brown wooden-cased clock sitting on the mantelshelf.

Punctuating the silence with a gentle ticking that echoed off the wooden floorboards at the pace of a restful heartbeat.

A rhythm that framed time, pulled your thoughts and words into its pulse if you listened to it. Never stopped.

Made you think in seconds.

A family heirloom ticking off the years. Beating out the rhythm of the generations.

It reminded Frank of his grandfather.

His grandfather. Old but upright. And tall, really tall. Looking down at him from under the thin white hair, sweeping him up into his arms, and marching around the sitting room singing 'Onward Christian Soldiers' – beating time with his hand on the seat of Frank's trousers.

And his grandfather would say…

169

"Look at that clock – there you are – 'What goes around comes around'."

"What goes around comes around." Frank had never really understood what he meant by that. It was just one of his grandfather's sayings. His grandfather had lots of sayings:

"Good better best, never let it rest,

Till your good is better, and your better best.

"That's what they taught us in school.

"Good better best, never let it rest

Till your good is better, and your better best."

He'd always said that one twice. Frank was never quite sure why.

His grandfather. Straight-backed and respectable. Never went out without his trilby hat, which he'd raise to any lady that he passed. Always reminiscing. Singing him snatches of old music-hall songs, songs that had been sung to him when he was a child.

Gilbert and Sullivan, adverts for Rington's tea and Woodbines. Frank could still sing them all now.

And the same memories. Wartime memories, told and re-told.

"That night we swam out to rescue those kids. We were on guard duty at the cliffs. Heard the shouting. Me and George and Eddie. The first day they'd been evacuated it was. City kids having a laugh. Having a laugh! They'd never seen the sea before and just kept walking out along the rocks. Wanted to get to the end of them. And then they looked round and there was just water behind them.

"One of them drowned. I had hold of him as well, but we kept going under the water, and when they pulled us out, he was gone. Must have been about ten. I'll never forget his face."

And, "But we were the lucky ones mind you." (Frank always mouthed that phrase with his grandfather – he knew when it was coming and he liked joining in. He always thought of his grandfather as 'one of the lucky ones'.) "We were the lucky ones. All those kids and their mothers – three hundred of them – at the pictures on a Saturday afternoon. All dead – hit by that bomb.

"And you know what film they were watching?"

Frank knew.

It was *It Could Happen to You!* Somehow the truth was always stranger than fiction.

His grandfather had been a drummer in a dance band. He'd played at the Baths Hall hops in the local towns.

"Real music in those days. Ten of us in the band. Thursday and Friday nights. And then on Saturdays one of the big bands would come to town. We'd just play for the beer. Swing, jive and waltzes. Music you could dance to. Music you could hear. Not like nowadays.

"And the halls would be packed out. They'd come in from the villages. Like Eddie – cycle ten miles, just to get to the dance he would. And he'd be up the next morning, seven o'clock – working in the blacksmith's.

"And we'd play that song. 'What goes around comes around'."

A different age.

His grandfather had died over thirty years go.

Frank looked again at the clock.

The rhythm seemed to be playing one of his grandfather's songs.

And the words of the song came flooding back. In his mind he could hear his grandfather's band and see visions of smoky dance halls. The couples clinging as they circled in the last dance of the evening.

> *When we look to the future, and dream all our dreams,*
> *Our plans and intentions, our hopes and our schemes,*
> *There are things to remember, lessons that last*
> *So much to be learned when we look to the past.*

171

Remember the good times, the things that we'd say
The stories we'd tell, the games that we'd play
They'll not be forgotten for there's one thing I've found
What goes around comes around.

Remember the places, the people we've met.
The songs that we've sung, that we'll never forget.
Remember the words and the memories abound
What goes around comes around.

He smiled at the corny words. "Songs are certainly not like that nowadays," he thought.

Certain images in his mind were inextricably linked to that song. The first time he'd heard it on the radio, sitting in his grandfather's front room. It always made him remember that room. The furniture – the pictures – the clock.

Frank closed his eyes.

'What goes around comes around.'

The noise of a throbbing bass intruded into his thoughts, charging the street outside with its drive and energy and excitement. He could hear the screamed words blasting into the night against a background of howling guitars.

'You never told me–'

There was a sudden explosion of noise.

His thoughts shattered as the windowpane behind him cascaded in across the room.

Shards of glass lacerated his face. A rough stone rolled across the carpet in front of him. He felt the blood dripping down his chin. Outside in the street, he could hear the immature voices of children.

The front door was shaking as fists pounded against it.

Voices called through the letterbox, "Please let us in!"

"We've come to say sorry."

He opened the door and the children crowded into the house – five or six of them.

They must have been about ten or twelve years old, mobile phones in hand, constantly checking the screens. Headphone earpieces led to hidden MP3s. They milled around the room.

"We didn't mean to. Sorry. We're really sorry."

"We were just having a laugh."

"It's okay," said Frank trying to watch them all at once. But there were too many of them. He felt helpless – out of control – just wanting them to go. After what seemed an age they finally trooped out and he slumped down in the chair again – and realized.

The clock was gone!

He could hear them shouting and running down the street.

"Loser."

He ran out of the house.

The gang was across the other side of the street. Running towards the bridge over the canal. Out of breath, along the street, he watched them disappear into the shadows of the footpath that ran down the steps and alongside the towpath.

And then in front of him there was a cry and a splash, as he watched the boy at the back of the group fall into the canal.

Frank threw himself into the water.

Black, cold, wet – mud and silt in his mouth. The blurred orange of the streetlight on the bridge mirrored in the water's broken surface. Dragging the boy's body, so heavy in the water, back to the canal bank. The song suddenly coming back into his mind.

'What goes around comes around.'

Hands pulling him. The boy choking and gasping. Blue lights. Offers of help. Silence.

Silence. Sitting once again in the front room of the house. Slumped in the chair, replaying the events of the evening over and over again in his mind. Glass still scattered across the carpet.

Silence. No reassuring rhythm.

Silence. Broken once more by the sound of throbbing bass speakers as a car slowed and then stopped outside the house. The sound that would now forever be linked to the events of that night.

Banging on the door. A boy's voice, shouting something through the letterbox.

"Please!"

173

He sat slumped in the chair. Not moving. The noise of the car roared away into the night.

The voice through the letterbox again.

"Please."

He lurched out of the chair, reached the front door and flung it open.

Nobody there. Aware of a small object at his feet, he looked down. On the doorstep, still ticking, sat the clock.

Author's note: the incidents related by Frank's grandfather actually took place during the Second World War and were reported in the newspapers at the time.

Learning through song

Using music to remember things by

Tim Harding

A good way to teach is by singing a song,
And if the tune's catchy you'll all sing along.
It's like visualization, it works just the same,
And it sorts information – it gives it a frame.

For there are clues there to help you, a tune and a beat,
We remember still better the things we repeat,
The things we repeat, time after time,
Supported by rhythm, and words that will rhyme.

And the type of the rhythm and tune that you choose
Are for catching the mood of the subject you use
And the instrumentation – the genre, the style
Makes you think, get excited and dance, or just smile.

175

Music surrounds us in our lives – it stirs the emotions, prompts our memories, and provides structures and frameworks for thought. It is a very natural form of communication, reflecting the vibrations and rhythms of the world around us, and it provokes responses in people of all ages. It encourages participation and enjoyment – prompting feelings of involvement (both emotional and kinesthetic) and togetherness.

Throughout our lives, we set words to music in chants and songs – from the playground with its clapping and skipping rhymes, to sports crowds using chants and familiar tunes to prove their allegiances and sense of unity, to religious meetings and rituals.

And whether we consider ourselves to be 'musical' or not, we all have a soundtrack to our lives. Songs sung to us in our childhood, songs and tunes from our record, CD and MP3 collections, and incidental music or advertising jingles heard on the radio or TV. We gather this aural collection in our minds and access it by prompts of words or images, and in a reciprocal way, these tunes and songs remind us of events and words experienced in our past.

It is well established that setting words to music can improve recall of those words and the use of song as an educational tool in the classroom has long been recognized. However, in recent years, in many of our schools, music has too often been seen exclusively as a discrete subject, with cross-curricular learning through song so often the preserve of the earlier years of our education system. While a topic work approach can encourage the linking of songs to work, particularly in the humanities, with the exception of modern foreign languages there has been all too little recognition of the value of using song as a serious teaching medium throughout the education system. Songs have had their place in the classroom but usually as an entity in themselves rather than as a vehicle for learning.

A song brings together a variety of elements, including rhythm, rhyme and repetition, which have all individually been proven to be excellent learning tools for all ages. The lyrics also constitute a body of information concisely and clearly organized into easily identified sections, which can be excellent for purposes such as the introduction of a topic, or indeed revision.

And because songs are such a good *oral* memory tool, they can be transmitted without the need for extended reading and writing. Songs therefore have a particularly beneficial impact on children who find reading difficult: their ability to recall facts is considerably improved through memory of tune rather than through memory of a body of written text.

To inform the future, we can look to the past. History has much to teach us about the efficacy of learning through song; modern teaching methods, which often have an emphasis on writing, have lost sight of the power of the oral tradition in its musical form. We need to rediscover the effect of music on thinking, memory, mood and communication, and to understand and realize the power of learning through song as an educational tool for the classroom, across the curriculum, and at all levels of our education system. We can hook into the enjoyment and fun of music and song – and because of its diversity, apply it in a style appropriate to the pupil.

For thousands of years songs have been used for a variety of purposes; informing and educating, entertaining, exhorting and persuading. From epic poetry and religious texts to short, snappy popular songs and even shorter advertising jingles, the emotional effect of music with its ability to stir and excite us, to calm or sadden us, has been linked with music's ability to lodge itself and its associated lyrics in our long-term memories. Folk dances, skipping rhymes and chants bear witness to the efficacy of simple actions to reinforce these elements.

In the oral tradition of many civilizations, tunes have been handed down the generations, and patterned language has often been set to music to assist the memory of tales and histories. Greek epic poetry was composed, rehearsed and performed orally with the metric structure as an aid to memory. The early English church realized the efficacy of song in teaching content and ritual – Bede in his *History of the English Church and People* tells how in 699 'the first singing-master in the Northumbrian churches was … invited from Kent … to teach the churches of the English the Catholic way of life'.

Lyric and song elements were also vital features of the English language during the medieval period, from the metrical structure of alliterative Anglo-Saxon poetry through to the rhyming poetry and lyrics of the later medieval ballads such as 'Sir Orfeo'. Other folk literature, from nursery rhymes and canter-fables (prose stories with repeated snippets of rhyme to join in with), to the extended songs and ballads of the seventeenth and eighteenth centuries, continued this oral tradition. Long, sung narrative ballads such as 'Chevy Chase' are known to have been popular for several centuries, the poem being linked to several different tunes during this time (Bruce and Stokoe, 1882). The complementary combination of rhythm, rhyme, song and story ensured that it was handed down from generation to generation. The recent upsurge of rap is, it could be argued, a renaissance of balladry – narrative lyrics with a strong cultural background embracing themes of everyday life and drama.

Educational applications from the Victorian classroom provide us with models and precedents for the use of rhythm in teaching and learning; the rote learning of facts such as multiplication tables were taught within a rhythmic structure and moral teaching was assisted by an abundance of rhymes & maxims:

> Good better best, never let it rest,
> Until your good is better, and your better best.

177

and

'Despise school and remain a fool.'

Advertising – from the street cries of traders to those involved in modern multimedia campaigns – has harnessed the effectiveness of music as a memory-aid: we know from our own experience that jingles and song lyrics are embedded in our long-term memory. The prompt of a word or words leads us to recall a phrase, slogan or lyric, often with its melody. Mention a particular product (think, 'Milky Bars'!) and we find ourselves humming the jingles heard in our childhood, some of which will stay with us for the rest of our lives.

We 'hang' information on clues and cues: a tune, a word, a picture. One element triggers the memory of another: 'Musical cues can trigger the recall of unique information that is difficult to retrieve using non-musical cues' (Rubin, 1977; Stewart and Punj, 1998). To understand this further we need to examine more closely the individual elements that make up the whole and give it its power: rhythm, rhyme, melody, repetition structure and mood.

The setting of words to rhythmic patterns gives them expression and emphasis, enhancing their meaning and impact. And the key to this is reliance on a steady beat or pulse. Songs have a consistent rhythm – which sets a pattern for our brain and this aids fluency of thought. Rhythm gives an expectation to the brain and even without the other elements of music, such as melody, our thought processes are assisted and we find ourselves remembering and repeating facts.

The 'High Scope' project discovered that, in young children, keeping a steady beat or 'beat competency' is thought to be one of the best predictors of later academic success (Kuhlman and Schweinhart, 1999). A steady beat also helps us to answer things as a group – we know when to give the response, and we have a precise time to process the information; the rhythm co-ordinates and unifies as we chant words and phrases together. The recitation of tables to a rhythm can lock these facts into our long-term memory. Often as we recall these, we find ourselves mentally chanting them to the rhythm. Rhythm also has links to kinesthetic learning. As we hear rhythmic sounds, we naturally want to join in by moving our bodies (watch an audience at a musical event tapping their feet, or clapping along to be part of the performance). Physical actions provide further reference points for the memory.

Rhyme is a key element of most song lyrics. It helps to define the rhythm and adds ornamentation to the words. End–rhyme provides a satisfying wholeness to a phrase, and is also very effective in providing predictive verbal clues. Internal rhyme provides further enrichment of expression. In education, particularly in Early Years teaching, the use of rhyme underpins both phonological and phonemic awareness, helping to develop

178

sensitivity to the patterns of language and especially to the patterns of written forms. Rhyme also gives us verbal clues that promote a sense of involvement as we spontaneously predict and join in – a regular feature of traditional storytelling. For example, if someone says 'and he huffed … and he puffed', you will naturally think 'and he blew the house down'. You may even say it out loud – children certainly do, given the prompt of the first line. And it's the aural clues and prompts that get children thinking in a discussion.

When teaching unknown songs, the rhyme can be used as a feature for prediction, comprehension and discussion. Saying a simple couplet and omitting the last word, and raising your voice towards the end of the second line, leads to spontaneous joining in. So, if in a KS2 class you say or write,

> 'Sentences look so much better, when they start with a ——'

everybody joins in with the requisite ending! And in a song about the water cycle, displaying the words

> 'We all need it (water) so we think it's great
> And it can even change its ——'[1]

and then asking the pupils to predict the final word can lead to valuable language work – and many suggestions involving scientific vocabulary.

Variation in the pitch of our voice is key to expression, and the sustained, patterned use of pitch is the basis of melody. Repeated melodies provide easily remembered patterning of thoughts, which can be associated with words – thus facilitating the recall of the words: 'An easy-to-sing melody further assists the memory of facts' (Roehm, 2001). Melody provides our brains with further clues; lyrics hang on to a tune, in the same way as visualization aids memory. Adding music to a set of words gives those words an extra dynamic which holds the words in our long-term memories.

There are a number of ways in which the structured organization of certain elements of sound repetition in language can assist memory storage and retrieval of a text or body of knowledge. At word level, repeated sound patterns, such as alliteration and rhyme, help us to notice particular words or phrases, and give them an added attractiveness to listen to, helping the fluency and impact of the song.

At phrase or sentence level, within a song, repeated words or phrases emphasize content. The chorus, or refrain, which often carries the main message, is repeated several times. A popular way of teaching songs is by rote, and the chunking of the song into musical phrases or lines. Once this has been repeated a few times it is lodged in our long-term memory.

179

At text level, 'Lyrics are remembered … when the song is heard more than once' (Calvert and Tart, 1993; McElhinney and Annett, 1996; Rainey and Larsen, 2002). Repetition and rehearsal of a song reinforce the memory of it. Modern strategies for promoting pop-songs often include several weeks of radio play before the release date to familiarize us with the song, and help us to remember it (and then hopefully buy it). If we hear or sing a song a number of times, its melody and lyrics are very effectively learned.

Song structure also adds to the effectiveness of rhythm and song in learning. 'Chunking' has long been seen as an effective memory technique. Breaking a long list of facts or a complicated piece of information into chunks helps us to visualize the data, and to organize the information in our minds. The organization of songs into verses and stanzas helps to 'chunk' information in an extremely effective way. The characteristics of some song structures are particularly effective. For example, choruses provide opportunities for repeating key information a number of times within a song. Each verse/section can focus on a specific and concise body of information, which can also be sequential – progressing from one concept/idea to the next.

Song structures also provide frameworks for creativity. They provide a brilliant opportunity to encapsulate what it is you want to teach within a particular type of structure. The song structure can also be related to the subject matter, and related writing genres. A complete song can cover complex material, organized to reflect the content – with a style and structure which could be, for example, chronological or logical, in a narrative structure, or following a methodology or process.

Music is also extremely diverse in its nature: it can create or reflect a wide spectrum of emotions and moods; and it may create a classroom climate conducive to learning by reducing stress levels and putting students at ease (Blanchard, 1979). It has the potential to improve students' interest in and attitude towards the material they are learning (Albers and Bach, 2003; Walczak and Reuter, 1994).

It can clearly be seen, therefore, that because of the advantageous combination of a variety of elements, music and specifically song is a most effective teaching medium. And yet it is not recognized as a valid teaching tool in many classrooms. Perhaps one reason for this under-use is a lack of confidence on the part of both teachers or pupils, possibly due to self-consciousness. A variety of strategies can help to surmount this problem.

Chants and raps are an excellent way into using music in the classroom – no singing is required. And when singing is introduced, it can be done to convincing backing-tracks, so that a plausible effect is almost instantly achieved. The focus should be on learning the content of the song, rather than on the vocal performance of the participants. Singing is such a valuable tool it is worth compromising quality of performance in favour of involvement. Good singing is certainly a skill to be developed and encouraged in the right context, but if the main learning focus of a lesson is science, an over-insistence on quality of performance will detract from the learning goal (perhaps in the same way that an over-emphasis on good handwriting can detract from creativity and content in writing).

It would be good to see, in the coming years, a resurgence of interest in the use of music and song in our schools as key tools for learning, not only because they encapsulate so many useful learning techniques, but also because they can engender a sense of excitement, creativity and fun – the best learning climate of all.

Notes

1   From 'Water Cycle Calypso': Tim Harding, *That's Science: Learning Science Through Songs*, Network Educational Press, 2003

Creating lyrics and songs: a practical guide

Tim Harding

Teachers of all musical abilities can use classroom songs, raps, rhymes and jingles. These can be

- self- or pupil-written, with or without melody
- self-written words, using a known tune
- purchased songs, written specifically for a purpose, for example, curriculum reinforcement and revision.

You can also add actions (either 'pat-a-cake'-type handclapping, other hand actions/hand jives or even simple or spontaneous dance moves – these are often volunteered by pupils!) as well as melodies, to make them even more memorable.

Write it yourself

Some of the best classroom rhymes and songs are those created by the teacher or pupils themselves. Often spontaneous, they have immediate relevance and ownership. They also raise the mood of a class. They're simple to construct – and fun! Use them for key learning objectives – or class conventions and rules or learning targets.

These are essentially words spoken or chanted to rhythm, with a rhyme to make them resolve, and can progress from simple phrases to couplets to four-line rhymes to complete songs/raps. To begin to create these start with a slogan or jingle.

Choose your words

The extraordinary stands out and so we notice and remember language which is patterned, or unusual or funny / rude when read or pronounced. To draw attention to key words and phrases in your teaching, use

- rhyme – 'notes can be quotes'

- alliteration – 'make neat notes!'

Add rhythm

Identify the key word or fact or phrase and put it into a relevant phrase that fits two counts of four beats when you tap or clap a steady pulse. Count to keep time. Fit a word to begin each beat. So in a KS2 lesson about story planning, keep a steady count of four and **clap on beats 1 and 3** as you say:

Count	**1**	2	**3**	4	**1**	2	**3**	4
	Where		When		Who		What	

Or for a maths/science lesson:

Count	**1**	2	**3**	4	**1**	2	**3**	4
	Twenty	four	hours	in	night	and	day	

While these could be used on their own, a two-line jingle is more satisfying; and a second rhyming line which develops or explains the first line will 'resolve' it. And so you can develop the first statement by saying:

Count	**1**	2	**3**	4	**1**	2	**3**	4
	Where		When		Who		What	

Count	**1**	2	**3**	4	**1**	2	**3**	4
	Setting		Time		Character		Plot	

or

Count	1	2	3	4	1	2	3	4
	Twenty	four	hours	in	night	and	day	

Count	1	2	3	4	1	2	3	4
	Earth	spins	round	in the	Sun's	bright	ray	

If you're working this out with a class, once you've got a basic couplet you can use this to discuss refinements using more complex language, so for instance you could replace 'spins round' with 'revolves'. A useful way of introducing rhyme-making to a class is to provide a first line and ask the pupils to think of the second line.

Ask them to suggest a response, or responses for this line (or make up your own):

	Pulls	and	push-	es	Make	things	go	
Count	1	2	3	4	1	2	3	4

Constructing a class rap or song lyrics

Structuring a rap or song

While there are many song structures, perhaps the simplest is the 4-bar verse, 4-bar chorus. Start with the subject content (use the 'Learning through song – song-building' content sheet on page 188).

1 First identify the main concept/area of knowledge – this could be your chorus. Write this together as a class shared exercise.

2 Ask pupils or groups to organize specific content into verses. You could give them a vocabulary list or ask them to suggest their own.

An example of this could be a song about parts of speech. Work on a chorus with two couplets about sentences. Then ask groups of pupils to write a couplet each about a specific element of a sentence (use the 'Rhyme or song frame – count of four' sheet on page 187 as a template): for example

    nouns   adjectives   verbs   conjunctions

Two of these can be combined for each verse. The completed song can have as many verses as you like! If pupils are confident, they can write whole verses (use the 'Song-building 4-line verse/chorus' sheet on page 189 as a template).

Rhythms for extended raps can be generated by clapping, tapping, and so on, or using the rhythm unit from an electronic keyboard or computer music software. There are many simple drum-sequencing programs available for use in the classroom. They are suitable for children from the Foundation Stage/Key Stage 1 upwards. Some mobile phones even incorporate simple sequencers that would provide a back-beat to raps. The structures can follow standard verse/refrain format.

Count	**1**	2	**3**	4	**1**	2	**3**	4
	......	......	......	......	......	......	......	......

Count	**1**	2	**3**	4	**1**	2	**3**	4
	......	......	......	......	......	......	......	......

Now sing it!

Adding the dimension of pitch and melody makes a rap more interesting and the melody can add a further memory hook.

Songs to tunes we know

This is a great way to use the lyrics you write yourself. Advantages include:

- Class/pupil sense of ownership.

- They are easy to join in with and pick up – everybody knows the tune already. All they need to feel involved is to learn the new words.

Tunes to use can include nursery rhyme tunes, adverts and pop songs. Because they all have very simple melodies and chord structures, they lend themselves to rewritten versions – and can be chosen appropriate to the age/musical tastes of the children involved.

A subject or phrase might suggest a song/tune you could use. For example, when a group of teachers were prompted with the phrase 'When Grandma went to the seaside', it led them to write a superb song based on the vocabulary/content of the KS1 History Unit 3 'What were seaside holidays like in the past?', using the tune of 'When Santa got stuck up the chimney'.

Sing these to your own accompaniment or none (!) or to karaoke-style backing tapes. Here are a few simple suggestions. For KS2, sing this couplet below to the tune of 'Twinkle, twinkle, little star':

> Sentences look so much better
> When they start with a capital letter.

185

You could even continue with:

> It will drive me round the bend
> If you don't put a full stop at the end!

One of the best simple songs to use is 'If you're happy and you know it', because this song has the third element – repetition. The principal learning objective is repeated three times – with a line in the middle for further explanation! Like this:

> For the area, times the base by the height,
> For the area, times the base by the height.
> The perimeter is found,
> If you go the whole way round,
> For the area, times the base by the height.

Or for Key Stage 3 pupils:

> Speed equals distance over time,
> Speed equals distance over time,
> If you really haven't got it,
> Just think S *(=) D
> iT ,
> Speed equals distance over time!

Or for the first part of the periodic table:

> Lithium, Sodium, Potassium, (Rubidium),
> Lithium, Sodium, Potassium, (Rubidium),
> Caesium, Francium,
> Caesium, Francium,
> Lithium, Sodium, Potassium, (Rubidium).

Some examples of educational lyrics set to modern pop songs and raps created by and for KS3 pupils can be found at www.songsforteaching.com

Writing your own music

Once the lyrics for a verse or chorus have been written, simple music can be added. A good way to start is by adding chords. Most keyboards have automatic chord settings, or you or a pupil may play the guitar. You could use combinations of chime bars (see below).

The 'three-chord trick' is the easiest combination. Many simple songs, including current pop songs, are based on the 'three-chord trick'.

- In the key of C: start and finish with the chord of C and also use the chords F and G.

- In the key of G: start and finish with the chord of G and also use the chords C and D.

Once a chord progression has been established, you can make up a melody either by singing or on instruments. Choose the musical style you want to give the right mood for your song.

Another useful musical structure is the 12-bar sequence (you'll recognize this from countless rock and roll, rock, and blues songs!). It involves six lines of two bars each (three rhyming couplets required). The chords are shown in the template below.

Rhyme or song frame – count of four

Subject

Content

Count	1	2	3	4	2	2	3	4
	......	......	......	......	......	......	......	......

Count	3	2	3	4	4	2	3	4
	......	......	......	......	......	......	......	......

Count	1	2	3	4	2	2	3	4
	......	......	......	......	......	......	......	......

Count	3	2	3	4	4	2	3	4
	......	......	......	......	......	......	......	......

Learning through song

Song-building content sheet

Subject:

Content/objectives – to reinforce learning of:

Vocabulary:

Main teaching point (chorus);

Specific teaching points:

Song-building 4-line verse/chorus

Subject

Content

Count	1	2	3	4	2	2	3	4
	......	......	......	......	......	......	......	......
Count	3	2	3	4	4	2	3	4
	......	......	......	......	......	......	......	......
Count	1	2	3	4	2	2	3	4
	......	......	......	......	......	......	......	......
Count	3	2	3	4	4	2	3	4
	......	......	......	......	......	......	......	......

Song-building 6-line verse/chorus

Subject

Content

Count	1	2	3	4	2	2	3	4
	......	......	......	......	......	......	......	......
Count	3	2	3	4	4	2	3	4
	......	......	......	......	......	......	......	......
Count	1	2	3	4	2	2	3	4
	......	......	......	......	......	......	......	......
Count	3	2	3	4	4	2	3	4
	......	......	......	......	......	......	......	......
Count	1	2	3	4	2	2	3	4
	......	......	......	......	......	......	......	......
Count	3	2	3	4	4	2	3	4
	......	......	......	......	......	......	......	......

189

12-bar song frame

Count	1	2	3	4	1	2	3	4
	C	/	/	/	C	/	/	/
	1	2	3	4	1	2	3	4
	C	/	/	/	C	/	/	/
	1	2	3	4	1	2	3	4
	F	/	/	/	F	/	/	/
	1	2	3	4	1	2	3	4
	C	/	/	/	C	/	/	/
	1	2	3	4	1	2	3	4
	G	/	/	/	F	/	/	/
	1	2	3	4	1	2	3	4
	C	/	/	/	C	/	/	/
					(or G)			

Success in the Creative Classroom: Using past wisdom to inspire excellence

References

Abbott, John and Ryan, Terry (2000) *The Unfinished Revolution*. Stafford: Network Educational Press.

Aitchison, Jean (1995) *Words in the Mind: An Introduction to the Mental Lexicon*. Oxford: Blackwell.

Albers, B. D. and Bach, R. (2003) 'Rockin' soc: using popular music to introduce sociological concepts', *Teaching Sociology*, 31(2): 237–245.

Aquinas, Thomas (1999) *Selected Writings*, ed. Ralph McInerny. London: Penguin.

Bellanca, James and Fogarty, Robin (1986) *Teach Them Thinking*. Arlington Heights, Illinois: Skylight Professional Development.

Bettelheim, Bruno (1976) *The Uses of Enchantment: The Meaning and Importance of Fairy Tales*. London: Penguin Books.

Blanchard, B. (1979) 'The effect of music on pulse rate, blood pressure and final exam scores of university students', *Journal of School Health*, 49(8), 470–471.

Bowkett, Stephen (1997) *Imagine That: A Handbook of Creative Learning Activities for the Classroom*. Stafford: Network Educational Press.

Bowkett, Stephen (2001) *ALPS StoryMaker: Using Fiction as a Resource for Accelerated Learning*. Stafford: Network Educational Press.

Bowkett, Stephen (2003) *Storymaker Catch Pack: Using Genre Fiction as a Resource for Accelerated Learning*. Stafford: Network Educational Press.

Brazier, David (2001) *Zen Therapy: A Buddhist Approach to Psychotherapy*. London: Robinson.

Bruce, J. Collingwood and Stokoe, John (1882) *Northumbrian Minstrelsy*. Newcastle upon Tyne: Society of Antiquaries, pages 1–24.

Calvert, S. L. and Tart, M. (1993) 'Song versus verbal forms for very-long-term, long-term, and short-term verbatim recall', *Journal of Applied Developmental Psychology*, 14(2): 245–260.

Caviglioli, Oliver and Harris, Ian (2004) *Reaching Out to All Thinkers*. Stafford: Network Educational Press.

Claxton, Guy (1998) *Hare Brain, Tortoise Mind*. London: Fourth Estate.

Egan, K. (1988) *Primary Understanding: Education in early childhood*. New York and London: Routledge.

Egan, Kieran (1989) *Teaching as Storytelling*. Chicago: University of Chicago Press.

Egan, Kieran (1997) *The Educated Mind: How Cognitive Tools Shape Our Understanding*. Chicago and London: University of Chicago Press.

Egan, Kieran (2002) *Imagination in Teaching and Learning*. London: Routledge.

Evens, Peter and Deehan, Geoff (1990) *The Keys to Creativity*. London: Grafton Books.

Franklin, James (1999) 'Diagrammatic reasoning and modelling in the imagination: the secret weapons of the Scientific Revolution', in G. Freeland and A. Corones (eds), *In 1543 and All That: Image and Word, Change and Continuity in the Proto-Scientific Revolution*. Dordrecht: Kluwer, pages 53–115.

Gardner, Howard (1993) *Multiple Intelligences: the theory in practice*. New York: Basic Books.

Goleman, Daniel (1996) *Emotional Intelligence: Why It Can Matter More than IQ*. London: Bloomsbury.

Greenfield, Susan (1997) *The Human Brain: a guided tour*. London: Phoenix (Orion).

Harding, Tim and Debbie Pullinger (2006) *Come Alive Stories*. (Yellow Door publications)

Harris, Judith Rich (1999) *The Nurture Assumption*. London: Bloomsbury.

Haward, Tom (2005) *Seeing History*. Stafford: Network Educational Press.

Hyerle, D. (1996) *Visual Tools for Constructing Knowledge*. Alexandria, Va: ASCD.

Jaynes, Julian (1990) *The Origin of Consciousness in the Breakdown of the Bicameral Mind*. London: Penguin Books.

Koestler, Arthur (1965) *Act of Creation*. London: Hutchinson.

Kuhlman, Kristyn and Schweinhart, Lawrence J. (1999) *Timing in Child Development*. Ypsilanti, Miss.: High/Scope Educational Research Foundation.

Langland W. (1959) *Piers the Plowman*. Trans. J. F. Goodridge. London: Penguin.

Lewis, B. and Pucelik, F. (1993), *Magic Of NLP Demystified: A Pragmatic Guide to Communication and Change*. Portland, Oregon: Metamorphosis Press.

McElhinney, M. and Annett, J. M. (1996) 'Pattern of efficacy of a musical mnemonic on recall of familiar words over several presentations', *Perceptal Motor Skills*, 82(2): 395–400.

Minshull, Steve (2000). *The Five Keys to Accelerated Learning*. Tring, Herts: Mind Motivation Ltd.

Milton, Richard (1994) *Forbidden Knowledge: Suppressed Research that could Change our Lives*. London: Fourth Estate.

Milton, Richard (1997) *Shattering the Myths of Darwinism*. Rochester, Vermont: Park Street Press.

Nelson, Leonard (1966) *Socratic Method and Critical Philosophy: Selected Essays*. New edn. Dover.

O'Connor, Joseph and Seymour, John (1990) *Introducing Neuro-Linguistic Programming*. London: Mandala.

Paley, Vivian Gussin (1986) 'On Listening to What Children Say', *Harvard Educational Review*, 56(2), pp. 122–131.

Paley, Vivian Gussin (1990) *The Boy Who Would be a Helicopter: The Uses of Storytelling in the Classroom*. Cambridge, Mass.: Harvard University Press.

Paley, Vivian Gussin (2004) *A Child's Work: The Importance of Fantasy Play*. Chicago: University of Chicago Press.

Plato (1929) *Epistles*, trans. R. G. Bury. London and New York: Loeb Classical Library, VII, 531.

Propp, Vladimir (2001) *Morphology of the Folktale*. Austin: University of Texas Press.

Rainey, David W. and Larsen, Janet D. (2002) 'The effect of familiar melodies on initial learning and long-term memory for unconnected text, *Music Perception*, 20(2): 173–186.

Rockett, Mel and Percival, Simon (2002) *Thinking for Learning*. Stafford: Network Educational Press.

Roehm, Michelle L. (2001) 'Instrumental vs. vocal versions of popular music in advertising', *Journal of Advertising Research*, May/June: 49–58.

Rose, Colin (1985) *Accelerated Learning*. Great Missenden: Topaz Publishing.

Rubin, D. C. (1977) 'Very long-term memory for prose and verse', *Journal of Verbal Learning and Verbal Behaviour*, 16: 611–621.

Sacks, Jonathan (2002) *The Dignity of Difference*. London: Continuum.

Saran, Rene and Neisser, Barbara (2004) *Enquiring Minds: Socratic Dialogue in Education*. Stoke: Trentham Books, SFCP and PPA.

Stewart, D. W. and Punj, G. N. (1998) 'Effects of using a nonverbal (musical) cue on recall and playback of television advertising: implications for advertising tracking', *Journal of Business Research*, 42: 39–51.

Tilling, Mike (2001) *Adventures in Learning*. Stafford: Network Educational Press.

Toffler, Alvin (1972) *Future Shock*. London: Pan Books.

Walczak, David and Reuter, Monika (1994) 'Using Popular Music to Teach Sociology: An Evaluation by Students', *Teaching Sociology*, 22(3): 266–269.

Wilson, Colin and Grant, John (eds) (1981) *The Directory of Possibilities*. London: Book Club Associates.

Zubrin, Robert (1996) *The Case For Mars: The Plan to Settle the Red Planet and Why We Must*. London: Simon and Schuster.

Index

Success in the Creative Classroom: Using past wisdom to inspire excellence